Saved, Adopted, Free:
Living the Romans 8 Life

Carl Smith

Saved, Adopted, Free: Living the Romans 8 Life

First Printing: 2021

All biblical references taken from ESV unless otherwise stated.

All stories are used with permission of those they involve, but some names have been omitted or changed.

ISBN: 9798578426919

DEDICATION

To my loving and supportive wife Linz and our beautiful children
Phoebe, Olivia, Toby & Abigail.

CONTENTS

ACKNOWLEDGEMENTS

I would like to thank all those who have helped me to write this book. To my family who have put up with me disappearing to write, especially to my wife, Linz, for supporting me in the process. Linz, your faith and commitment to Jesus are a constant source of inspiration to me, and I am delighted to have you as my bride and the mother to our four beautiful children. It is a pleasure to minister alongside you.

Thank you to those who read this book in its infancy. Special thanks to Linz, Ben, Rick, Kerry, Gemma, Peter, Fae and Jon. Thanks for encouraging me but also being honest enough to say what had to go from the first draft – and for helping to remove many grammatical errors. Special thanks to Jim for taking time at a busy time of year to read the book and write the foreword, and for your support generally in the process.

Thank you also to the people of St Mary's, Slaugham and St Mark's, Staplefield. It is a pleasure to minister alongside you and I appreciate the support you have given to me in the writing process.

Ultimate thanks and praise go to God – the true author – who has inspired me on what seems like a daily basis and is the constant source of my worship. I have grown closer to you through the writing of this book and I offer it back to you to do with as you like. Thank you, Jesus, for saving me and bringing me into relationship with the perfect heavenly Father.

FOREWORD

I am one of those people who struggle to know what to order when they are sat in a restaurant. The problem is, I like to eat…. everything. I read through the menu and if it were at all possible, both in terms of budget and health, I would eat it all. In my ideal scenario, what I'd really like, is to be able to have a little taster of everything that was available.

For me, Romans chapter 8 is similar. Where do you start? It's packed full of such incredibly rich truth and content. It can appear overwhelming. Familiar Bible verses that carry such power roll off the tongue: 'Therefore, there is now no condemnation for those who are in Christ Jesus….', 'The Spirit you received does not make you slaves, so that you live in fear again; rather, the Spirit you received brought about your adoption to sonship…', 'And we know that in all things God works for the good of those who love him…', 'What, then, shall we say in response to these things? If God is for us, who can be against us?'.

What Carl has done, through this book, is give us a taster menu of Romans 8. He has taken these incredible truths and reflected on them in a way that is both personal and powerful. We get to 'taste' the goodness of these words and as we do we develop a fuller understanding of who God is, who we are as His children and what it means to be adopted into His family - something we all need to grasp to a greater degree.

The great preacher Martin Lloyd Jones once said about Romans chapter 8 that 'The great theme is the security of the Christian'. This is something we all need to know so let me encourage you to read this book, reflect on these truths, let your heart be filled and your mind renewed.

I know Carl and I know that what he has written is also what he lives through his life, his family and his ministry. He has tasted all that Romans chapter 8 is offering, and he invites us to do the same. Enjoy!

Jim Partridge

PREFACE

When I first drafted this book, it was my intention to methodically work through Romans 8, one verse at a time. What I discovered, however, is that whilst Paul's flow is logical and methodical in the context of his letter, unpacking each verse in order didn't work in the context of a book. This book was never designed to be a Bible commentary, so a different approach was needed.

As I was editing the second draft, I realised that the verses I had selected to write about (which only form a small part of Romans 8) fell into three main sections, which have now formed the sections of this book. As a result, as you read you will discover that the verses do not go in the order that Paul has written them.

I do highly recommend reading Romans 8 in its entirety before reading any more of this book, to see how Paul's flow of writing teaches the truths that it does. I hope very much that this book will enhance your reading of Romans 8, in a way that writing it has done for me.

INTRODUCTION

A number of years ago there was an advertising campaign for a major supermarket brand. The challenge to the viewer was to sum up Christmas in just three words. Various lists were presented until at the end of the advert we were encouraged to believe that Christmas was best summed up by the name of that particular supermarket chain. Many preachers have since incorporated that advert into Christmas sermons and are clever enough to say it is better summed up in three-word phrases such as 'Jesus is born' or 'God with us'.

I wonder if you were to sum up your Christian identity in three words, what words would you use? There's no point me listing options as it is clear from the title of this book what I think the answer should be. These three words – saved, adopted, free – define what I believe a Christian to be and is the message of the whole gospel. I also think that the best summary of these three words, and what they mean for a Christian, can be found in the words of Romans chapter 8.

I am not one for choosing one particular Bible verse over another. I believe that all scripture is of equal importance and validity. I believe that God can and does speak to us and teach us about himself, ourselves and our relationship with Him through any passage that He chooses, even genealogies or seemingly repetitive texts about temple buildings. Whilst holding this view, I also suspect that many people who love the word of God will have parts of the Bible that they frequently come back to. Perhaps individual verses that have meant a lot, passages and verses that have been given prophetically, ones that challenge us and remind us of something we know we need to be doing for God, gospel stories that remind us of all that Jesus has done for us, or even stories that we remember from our childhood. Preachers who read this book may have those passages that they will preach from whenever they are asked to preach somewhere new. Some of these well-loved passages may be for a season, others for a lifetime of faith; I have no doubt that we all have them.

This, I believe, is a perfectly natural thing, because whenever we come to God's word we are approaching a relatable and personal God who knows us better than anyone else does, even better than we know ourselves. A God who knows what we need and when we need it, and who knows that we can often find what we need in His word, whether for ourselves or for others.

Although I said that I am not one for choosing one particular part of the Bible, I am still often drawn to Romans. It is a letter in the Bible that I come back to time and again. Romans is defined by Timothy Keller as 'the most sustained explanation of the heart of the gospel, and the most thrilling exploration of how that gospel goes to work in our hearts'.[1] J.I. Packer summed up Romans saying that 'All roads in the Bible lead to Romans, and all views afforded by the Bible are seen most clearly from Romans'.[2] It is a letter that has been the basis of entire reformations within the life of the Church. It is also a letter that has meant a great deal to me personally through many seasons of my life.

Right within the heart of Romans sits one chapter, that for me personally has had a profound effect. It is a chapter I return to regularly to develop my faith and fuel my ministry; one I teach from regularly and use to remind myself of my identity as a child of God. It has been said that if Romans is the Himalayas of the New Testament then chapter 8 is its Mount Everest. This one chapter of the Bible says so much about our faith, our status and our identity. Identity is something that many people struggle with, and to truly accept the biblical revelation that we are a people who are saved, adopted and free is a message that I feel is really needed in this generation, perhaps more so now than ever before. I often think that if every Christian could fully understand and grasp what Paul teaches in this chapter, then the world, and the universal Church, would be a very different place.

Most people would find it hard to argue with the fact that there is a need for people outside of the Church to know their identity – it is something that is so often impacted or affected by wrong things. So much of popular culture, in particular social media, revolves around people searching for their identity in being accepted – by a panel of judges, by the viewing public, or by their peers. We see it in everyday life and some of the things that people allow to shape their identity can lead to dangerous and damaging consequences. What some Christians fail to recognise is that once a person has had their life changed by Jesus, there is a new identity to be found in that relationship but often that identity still needs to be uncovered and discovered. In my years within the church, I have encountered so many Christians who perhaps know and accept that Jesus died for them, have surrendered to their need of Him to be saved and for forgiveness, and yet for years have struggled to fully accept their identity as children of God, heirs of the Kingdom, chosen, adopted, adored and unconditionally loved by the God of the universe, the one in whose image they are made. This acceptance is a process that we need to be intentional about. There is also a key role that the Holy Spirit plays in our acceptance of that identity that can often be forgotten or lost – all of this can be found in Romans chapter 8.

You will find in this book that the message of the whole gospel is repeated a lot, as it is indeed in much of Paul's writing. I make no apology for that. The knowledge and acceptance of the full gospel is something that is not only for those yet to be saved but is also something that those who have been saved need to be reminded of often. If you ever find yourself feeling tired of hearing the gospel then something needs to change – the gospel should never be boring to us, and we should be reminding ourselves of the life-changing truth within it on a daily basis. By 'gospel' I mean the whole of scripture that points to Jesus. The gospel is so much more than the story of salvation, as important as that is. It is only when we grasp the full gospel, as summarised so beautifully and powerfully by Paul in Romans, that we can fully understand our status before God.

To quote Packer again, '…when the message of Romans gets into a man's heart there is no telling what may happen'.[3] This book uses Romans chapter 8 and some of its key themes as a springboard to really understand what it means to be saved, adopted and free.

SAVED

1 NO CONDEMNATION

There is therefore now no condemnation for those who are in Christ Jesus

-8:1-

We all have moments of our past that we are not proud of. Those times when we have done something out of character, the memory of which still haunts us today. These memories can play over and over again in our minds as we think about how we could have done things differently. If they are moments from our childhood we may think how different it would have been if, knowing what we know now, we did things again.

I had a friend at school who was a great kid. He rarely set a foot wrong. He was loved by all the teachers and students alike. He was a hard worker and was very talented in many ways. There was one time, however, that he and I did get into trouble for talking during a class. He had never experienced the wrath of a teacher before, and as we were (unjustly in my opinion) handed our detention cards, I could see his face fall. He had never experienced this feeling before, at least not in school. He had been passed a judgement by a teacher. He tried to protest it, but could quickly see that doing so was only going to make matters worse. Whether we had caught the teacher on a bad day, whether or not that teacher was in the right, the detention had been given, the judgement had been passed. I distinctly remember talking to him after the lesson. This was a first detention for both of us and neither of us knew how our parents would respond to the news of it. Although we would not have had the language for it at the time, I think we both expected condemnation, for the decision of the school to be enforced by our parents, to receive judgement from them as well as the teacher. In reality, neither of us received that. My friend's parents tried to contest the decision, using his otherwise faultless record as their reasoning, and my parents saw it as an opportunity for me to learn from a mistake, but neither of us received the condemnation that we perhaps expected.

Although this is a small example (there are probably much more significant ones that I could give), I would imagine we all know what it feels like to be condemned, and hopefully we can all give examples of times when we expected to receive condemnation but were surprised and delighted when we did not. It is something that Paul and Jesus both address in much of their teaching and so is an important place from which to begin this book, but Romans 8:1, as we will discover, sits within a much wider context.

The Himalayas

The opening verse of Romans 8 instantly shows why this whole chapter is such a good summary of the gospel. The opening words of Romans 8 are full of encouragement, power and so much hope. This takes on more life when we see it in the context of the first seven chapters, and even more so when put in the context of the whole of the Old Testament and any others texts that would have been available to Paul at the time. Add to that, the context of the gospel, and Paul's own life experiences.

It is clear to me that Paul has an aim in writing Romans, to what has become a divided church: to remind them of the gospel, and in so doing, to strengthen their understanding of what it means to identify as followers of Jesus Christ. Any good commentary on Romans would give a detailed overview of Paul's opening chapters but in brief summary: Paul speaks of deep and theological issues that he is keen for the Church to grasp and to approach with a level of simplicity. He covers themes of guilt, righteousness, Jewish relationship to the law, faith, and lessons from well-known historical figures (drawing from his own Jewish background). He covers the theme of justification, and even goes back to the beginning of humanity. He speaks about marriage as an example of commitment to the Lord, and about baptism and resurrection. Throughout, he is using terms and language that would have been very familiar to the Jewish people and to their own history and their relationship with God, but he is bringing that language into the light of Christ. In doing this, Paul is showing that what Jesus does for our relationship with God is both a fulfilment and a new thing, a new covenant, a new promise, that paradoxically also fulfils the promises of old.

Immediately before chapter 8, Paul uses his own personal struggles and experiences to teach the reader about the inner battle that we as followers of Jesus can all face at times. He uses those well-known (and if we are honest, very comforting) words: 'For I do not do the good I want, but the evil I do not want is what I keep on doing...' (7:19). In doing this, he is acknowledging that it is likely to be the experience of the people of Israel and for all the individuals who would have been hearing these words read in their fellowship gathering, as is true of all people who live in this world. It is a common battle for all have who desire to be better versions of themselves because of what Jesus has done for them.

In chapter 8 then, Paul is saying (to paraphrase): 'in light of all of this' or 'with all of this truth in mind' or perhaps even 'because of the grace of the God who is the author and perfecter of all that I have been teaching you…'. There is now no condemnation for those who are in Christ Jesus, and that is true even though we are still struggling with that battle between the flesh and the spirit. This is why it is important for us to *know* it as a truth and not just to *feel* that it is true.

Condemnation

The word 'condemnation' is not a word we use very much in our daily vocabulary. It is a word that tends to have a very negative connotation. Although we don't use the word much, condemnation is something that we see happening on an almost daily basis, as we see people judging others, condemning the behaviour of certain people groups, and making quite final decisions about certain things. Paul was certainly not afraid to use it. In fact, the word condemnation appears over sixty times in the New Testament, the majority of these times in Paul's writings.

'Condemnation' is a term that has to do with judgement and can refer to the act of judgement in the court of law and in particular the consequences of that judgement. This is why today you may hear the term 'condemned to x number of years in jail'. There is a finality that is associated with it. If a building is condemned then a decision has been passed that it is no longer fit for use. What Paul is saying in Romans 8 is that due to all that Jesus has done on the cross, and not because of anything we have done, there is no consequence of judgement on us. Ultimately, Jesus bore that consequence for us; what was marked as condemned and no longer fit for purpose, has been restored, renewed and made new again.

This is essential because before Jesus died for our sins, we were a people who deserved condemnation and the cause of that condemnation was our sin. Whilst my friend at school may come across as being perfect (having only had one detention in his whole time at secondary school), the reality is he wasn't, because none of us are. As Paul highlights earlier in his letter '...all have sinned and fall short of the glory of God...' (3:23). He is saying that there has to be a consequence to that sin; sin has to be punished, and we, as bearers of that sin, deserve punishment too. In dying on the cross, we know that Jesus took that punishment on our behalf. Once we accept what Jesus has done for us we are acquitted and declared righteous in God's sight – not a righteousness earned by the law but given by the grace of God (see Romans 3:19-26). In God's eyes, there is no condemnation.

Jesus himself teaches on this theme. In John chapter 5, in response to Jesus being rebuked for healing on the sabbath, Jesus is teaching about life in Him and His relationship with the Father and the reason for His coming. Then He hits his readers with this: 'I tell you the truth, whoever hears my word and believes in Him who sent me has eternal life and will not be condemned...' (vs 24 – NIV). You also find this truth in the verse following the most famous verse in the world. People will often quote John 3:16, not realising that the incredible life-changing truth for us is actually found in verse 17 where Jesus declares: 'For God did not send His son into the world to condemn the world, but in order that it may be saved through Him. Whoever believes in Him is not condemned...'. Jesus Himself has said that there is no condemnation for those that are in Him and who choose life with Him! He does make it clear that condemnation is still there for those who choose not to accept Him, but for those who have accepted Jesus' sacrifice and made the transaction of sins for His forgiveness, there is no condemnation. We are free from judgement. Whilst we may still fear judgement, and fear its consequences for others, we are free from it because that condemnation has been removed, revoked, rescinded for good!

The fact that God has made this possible is the greatest miracle of all – that He has dealt with our sin *because* of His love for us. God's love for us moved Him to punish the sin, to remove the condemnation. The reality is that God abhors sin and He had to see it punished. His desire is to have a loving relationship with us, but in order to protect what He loves He has to destroy the power of what He hates – and that is our sin. This is what Jesus did on the cross – He destroyed the power of sin, and then ultimately, through the resurrection, He destroyed the main consequence of that sin, which is death. It is only because of this that there is no condemnation for those who are in Christ Jesus.

When you look at the life of Jesus and how He interacted with sinners and people regarded by society and religious leaders as 'unclean', you see what it looks like for there to be no condemnation. Take, for example, Jesus' encounter with the woman caught in adultery. Having challenged the crowd who were looking to stone her to reflect on their own sin before judging hers, He creates an environment in which no judgement of another can be made by anyone other than Him. Leaders and onlookers have skulked away knowing that they cannot possibly say that they have no sin, and therefore have no right to judge that of another. The only person left with any right to judge is Jesus. Whilst He does challenge her sin and He does urge her to go away and sin no more, the one thing He does not do is condemn her. She receives grace, pardon, forgiveness, hope and love but she does not receive even a hint of condemnation (see John 8:1-11).

Consider the story of Jesus meeting Zacchaeus, the hated and unpopular tax collector who has been living a life of dishonesty. Jesus chooses to show him honour and love by asking to spend time with him and to eat with him, much to the disapproval of the crowd. Time with Jesus leaves Zacchaeus changed; he shows a desire for repentance and he rights the wrongs he has made. Zacchaeus gets a second chance, a new start, but what he does not receive from Jesus is condemnation (see Luke 19:1-10).

Jesus encounters a woman at a well, who is an outcast of her own society for reasons that Jesus reveals prophetically during their conversation. She is an outcast, due to her messed-up life, who is likely to be drawing water in the heat of the day in order to avoid contact with other people. The Messiah reveals her past, challenges her present, and gives her a hope for her future – but there is no condemnation (see John 4:1-42).

God has fought for what He loves by destroying what He abhors. That is the power of the cross. This is what frees us from condemnation. It is because He has taken our punishment on our behalf that we no longer have to fight evil in the same way; we can combat sin with love and forgiveness, a new way shown by Jesus, because He has destroyed the power sin has over us, allowing us to rise above it with love. There is now NO condemnation for those who are in Christ Jesus!

In Christ

It is amazing how many people quote 'there is now no condemnation' and forget that this is a truth only for those who are 'in Christ Jesus'. It is an unusual expression but it is not a concept that is unique to Romans. Paul uses this thought in a similar way in Galatians 2:17-20: 'But if, in our endeavour to be justified in Christ, we too were found to be sinners, is Christ then a servant of sin? Certainly not! For if I rebuild what I tore down, I prove myself to be a transgressor. For through the law I died to the law, so that I might live to God. I have been crucified with Christ. It is no longer

I who live, but Christ who lives in me. And the life I now live in the flesh I live by faith in the Son of God, who loved me and gave himself for me.'

This passage in Galatians 2 shows the kind of transformation that takes place when we make that decision to say our 'yes' to Jesus. When we acknowledge that we were crucified with Christ, He takes up residence in our lives. That is quite a change. This is a truth of the gospel that many people struggle to fully grasp, comprehend or live out, but it is essential in our understanding of the transformative power of the gospel.[4] The term 'in Christ' is, more often than not, the term that is used in the New Testament to describe a Christian, and so understanding this phrase is important in our discovery of our Christ-like identity.

Jesus also made it clear in John 14 that it was very much His desire that those who choose life with Him are found 'in Him' as He is in the Father. To be 'in Christ' is to have our entire identity in the person of Jesus Christ, and in our relationship with Him. This is a concept that many people, even many Christians, can find extremely difficult to grasp. It concerns me how many churches I have been involved in where there seems to be a huge, and often deep-rooted, need to *earn* God's love and acceptance, through any manner of things. The people in these places may think they know and understand that they can't earn salvation but despite this you will often find people who are exhausted from trying to earn God's approval, to be loved more, to be more acceptable to God or trying to be a 'better Christian'. This is a terrible lie of the enemy, and a theme that will be explored further in another section of this book.

We have to ask here: 'What makes a Christian a Christian?' With some other religions, you could describe a person from that religion by what they do, by how they practice their faith, by what they stand for, by what they claim, by what they teach, and even, in some cases, by where they come from. For the Christian, however, the answer is not wholly found in any of those. The reason it can't be found in those things, is that the heart of Christianity is not religion, practices, rules, regulations, or 'the law'. At the heart of Christianity is a relationship with the person of Jesus Christ. This Jesus, the Son of the living God, has done everything to restore a relationship between the creator and His creation. Jesus has done it all. We no longer have to perform to earn His love. We no longer have to work for His approval. His love and His approval have been sealed and secured by the blood of Jesus on the cross and made eternal by His resurrection and ascension. As Tullian Tchividjian states, 'Our standing with God is not based on our ongoing struggle for Jesus but on Jesus' finished struggle for us.'⁵

This is a truth that so many people seem to miss or at least fail to fully grasp. The gospel shows us that Jesus is the perfect, and only, antidote for our sinful nature. He has dealt with the barrier between us and God once and for all on the cross. So, if we fall short, if we mess it up, if we get caught up in sin (which we will), He has dealt with the eternal consequences of that. Yes, we still have to face up to consequences. Yes, our sin will still have an impact on our daily lives. The difference, however, is that we are no longer *defined* by that sin. Our identity then is not in sin (as it was before) but is in the person of Jesus Christ. We are found to be in Him and He is found to be in us. This relationship defines who we are. In the moment you accept Jesus into your life, that moment when you say 'Yes' to Him, that moment when you choose repentance and life in Him, the old self is put to death (see Romans 8:13), and new life is formed (see John 3). As you are filled with the Holy Spirit (see Romans 7:6), your very identity is changed. You are still you, you will still have likes and dislikes, you will even probably still have the same weaknesses and vices (unless God intervenes supernaturally), but your identity is no longer to be found in those things, rather it is found in the person of Jesus as you are adopted into the family of God. The God who accepts you without condemnation. The God who accepts you despite your past, even despite the things you may still be struggling with today. This freedom from condemnation comes with no conditions other than saying 'Yes' to Jesus.

The whole concept of being 'in Christ' is more central to understanding who we are than many people seem to realise, hence why Paul uses it in his central point in Romans. If you ever find yourself striving in any way for God's approval, or seeking to earn your 'Christian identity', if you ever find yourself trying to prove your Christianity to others by activity or service, then it could be that you haven't fully grasped this concept. Somewhere, somehow, perhaps gradually over time, you may have struggled to accept the fact that because Jesus succeeded you are now in Him, and your failure has no bearing on your God-given identity. Mistakes, giving into sin, struggling with depression or anxiety or struggling with finances or relationships do not change the fact that you are in Christ and that He is in you. If you are a Christian, then your identity is firmly rooted in Christ's accomplishment on the cross.

Knowledge and acceptance of this truth can lead to true freedom. Paul was desperate for the people of Rome to truly grasp this concept. People had been placing their identity in all kinds of things that on the surface appeared good. Many of them were struggling to understand or accept their new-found identity as followers of Jesus, but he wanted them to understand that there really is **no condemnation** for those who are **in Christ Jesus**. The rest of this powerful chapter in Romans moves on to explore this liberating truth and its impact on our lives.

Lord, thank you for dying for me. Thank you for taking the punishment I deserve so that there is no condemnation for me. Help me to fully grasp what it means for you to live in me and me in you, that I may intentionally choose to remain in you always. Amen!

2 FUTURE GLORY

For I consider that the sufferings of this present time are not worth comparing with the glory that is to be revealed to us.

-8:18-

For much of human history there has been a fascination with the future. For years, sci-fi writers and comic book creators have sought to imagine what the future may be like. I love looking today at some of the predictions from twenty or thirty years ago about what the 2000s would be like, and to see how, although some got some things right, others were way off in their predictions (personally I am still waiting for a hoverboard as predicted in *Back to the Future*). Equally, I have no doubt that there is technology that exists today that not even the most visionary sci-fi writer could have imagined would be possible. Early inventors thought that there would never be a need for every home to have a computer, and yet here we are today with not only computers in the home, but laptops, tablets and many phones that are more capable than early computers.

When Paul speaks of future glory, he is not writing about technological or even human advances. He is not talking about the improvement of quality of life, or of scientific discovery. Paul knows that the one thing we can't do is predict the future; even Jesus couldn't do that (see Matthew 24:36). He is writing, instead, of something that is far more certain than any of that. Whilst we can't predict the future of this earth and what will happen on it, we can, as Christians, be certain of our future hope, and having a certainty about our future should make a huge difference to our life in the present.

Promises, Promises

When promises are made and then broken, the impact can be huge. Trust is broken every time a promise is not kept, which can have a lasting effect on any relationship, be it political or personal. Politicians are renowned for making promises. The sad reality is that they are just as renowned for breaking them. When they do lie, the people whom they are called to lead can lose confidence not only in them as people, but in severe cases, they can lose faith in the entire regime, policies or values. That lost trust then needs to be (often slowly) regained, and in some cases that can take a lifetime. This is why, as a church leader, I often speak about intentions rather than promises. I never know when other circumstances may make it impossible for me to do what I aim to do. It is important to avoid making promises if we are not 100% sure that they can be kept – which is rarely, if ever, the case.

The contrast to this is the fact that there are over 3,000 promises made by God in scripture, though some of those promises, granted, are yet to be fulfilled (such as His return and restoration of all things). Out of the rest, not a single one has been broken – not a single one! That, in my mind, is a pretty good track record of promise keeping. When God promised Abraham that he would be the father of many nations (Genesis 17:4-5) He made sure, against all human odds and possibilities, that He made that happen. When God promised Noah (with the rainbow as a reminder) that He would never again flood the whole earth (Genesis 9:11-13), we find thousands of years later that He has kept that promise. When He promised a land to His chosen people (Exodus 3:17) He provided it, even if it took longer than they would have liked (see the book of Joshua).

Ultimately, when God promised to send a Saviour (Isaiah 19:20) to set His people free, He sent Jesus as the fulfilment of that promise. He did so in exquisite detail. He promised that the Saviour would be born in Bethlehem (Micah 5:2), so he caused a census to happen so that Mary and Joseph would be forced to travel to where Joseph was from, which 'just so happened to be' Bethlehem. Everything from who would announce the Messiah, to where and how He would arrive, and what message He would bring, was promised by God and fulfilled in Jesus.

Jesus himself was the best at promise making and keeping too. Before He died, He promised He would be back; three days later, promise fulfilled. He promised His disciples the gift of the Holy Spirit; the incredible, life-changing experience of those same disciples during Pentecost is the fulfilment of that promise. He promised Peter that He would build His church and years later the church is born and begins to spread the news of Jesus on a global scale. He is still building His church today.

All of this, alongside all the other promises that He made, can give us absolute confidence that when God makes a promise to His people, He is going to keep it. He can't not keep it – promise keeping is in His very nature, so to break a promise would be to deny a part of who He is. When Jesus says these words in Matthew 19:28 – 'Truly, I say to you, in the new world, when the Son of Man will sit on his glorious throne, you who have followed me will also sit on twelve thrones...' and in the following verse '...everyone who has left houses or brothers or sisters or father or mother or children or lands, for my name's sake, will receive a hundredfold and will inherit eternal life', we can be certain that we can trust such words, because they are promises being made by the world's *only* true promise keeper.

Jesus made it clear that we simply won't know when this is going to be (though some people still try to predict it), but we can know that it *will* happen. Jesus says that He will return (see Matthew 25:31-46), so we can trust that He will be back. Paul is so clearly certain about this fact that he speaks with absolute confidence about a day which makes everything we face in life now, with its joys and struggles, pale into insignificance. Let's not forget that Paul wrote these words long before the book of Revelation existed so he is not using that prophetic vision as his basis for this teaching. Paul's certainty doesn't come from a knowledge of what the future holds but from a relationship with the one who holds the future, and the promises Jesus made.

Glory

That future of our eternity is certain, and so is what that future holds for us. It holds a glory, the likes of which will be incomparable to anything this world has to offer. Glory is a term that is often used out of context, or at least with a misunderstanding of its proper meaning. People might chant 'glory, glory…' to their football teams from the stands, we might give glory to someone who has achieved something amazing and some may even strive for such glory – but glory was not intended to be ascribed to human beings, at least not for anything that we achieve in our strength. We were not created to find or to achieve our own glory. It was never God's intention for us to manufacture our own glory, but rather to ascribe it to Him, the only one truly worthy of it. By His grace, however, He has also designed us with the idea that we share in His glory. In order to fully grasp how much of a miracle and blessing it is that we can share in His glory, it helps to understand what glory truly is.

When we see the glory of God in the Old Testament it is often not a pretty sight. When the people of Israel have an encounter with the glory of God they often end up face down on the ground (Numbers 20:5, Leviticus 9:24, Genesis 17:3, 1 Kings 18:39 – to name just a few examples). If people did not fall prostrate on the ground they were, at the very least, terrified by the experience (Genesis 28:17). In the book of Hebrews, the writer is reflecting back on the life of Moses and states: 'Indeed, so terrifying was the sight that Moses said, "I tremble with fear"' (Hebrews 12:21). Even creation itself trembles at the glory of God. Psalm 77:16 says 'The waters saw You O God, they were in anguish; The deep waters also trembled.' When we read of Isaiah's encounter with the glory of God, it is easy to remark upon his response when he is made aware of his own unholiness, but even more striking than that is the fact that even the angels surrounding him are having to cover their faces at the sight of God's glory (Isaiah 6:2). We also see this happening in Revelation: in 7:11 we are given a picture of the throne room of heaven where 'all the angels were standing around the throne and around the elders and the four living creatures; and they fell on their faces before the throne and worshipped God'. God's glory is not something to be taken lightly and has never been something to a provoke a minimal, quiet, gentle response. God's glory is something we, as His children, are yet to experience fully. Whilst we may occasionally have glimpses of it, they are only glimpses. The book of Revelation gives us a picture, but it is hard to really imagine what it will truly be like. Scripture simply teaches us that it will be glorious.

Glory to Glory

Remarkably, God does not want us to have our own glory because He knows that what He has for us is far greater than any glory we could ever seek for ourselves. He has for us a share in 'His own glory' (2 Peter 1:3). Paul explains this in 2 Corinthians when he says 'And we all, with unveiled face, beholding the glory of the Lord, are being transformed into the same image from one degree of glory to another. For this comes from the Lord who is the Spirit' (2 Corinthians 3:18). This isn't the kind of glory that makes us look good, this is the kind of glory that shows God off to the world, and this is done through us being made in the image of the God of glory. As those who are made in His image, and adopted by Him in Jesus, we are able to approach Him and to be in relationship with Him. This is powerfully symbolised with the curtain tearing in two violently during the crucifixion of Christ. What was previously the holy of holies, reserved for the priest alone, is now an open invitation into a relationship with the God of all glory.

Sharing in this glory and becoming people of that glory shows that we have a father who is proud of us and wants to show us off because He can now be seen in those who have the Spirit of God dwelling in them. This was always His intention for the people of Israel but they all too often failed to reflect His glory. In fact, as Paul highlights at the beginning of his letter to the Roman church, it has always been God's intention for us to share in His glory but we 'exchanged the glory of the immortal God for images resembling mortal man' (1:23). We continue to make that exchange, and in so doing we fail, on an all too regular basis, to represent Him as well as we could. However, His glory then abounds in us as we discover His mercies are new every morning, as we model a life of being forgiven and forgiving others, as our humanity is being sanctified by the life-giving Spirit at work in us and through us, to the honour and glory of God's name.

When we share in God's glory, the irony is that we don't become beneficiaries of that glory, but He does. The one who deserves all the glory is glorified in and through us. We cannot obtain this kind of glory by doing more, serving more, giving more, or striving more. This glory is a direct result of living in the presence of God and the presence of God living in us. This was true of Moses when he came down from the mountain. The glory seen on and in him was a direct result of having been in the presence of the God of glory (Exodus 34:29-35). Whenever we get it wrong or we mess up, His glory is still seen through the grace we receive, and when we get it right, His glory is seen by the changes in us as we seek to be more like Him – so either way God gets the glory when we choose to share in it. The main way God's glory is displayed is in the same way Jesus displayed it most – in and through self-sacrificial love. This is why glory is never truly about us, but all about Him. The moment we seek that glory for ourselves, or we try to achieve it on our own, the more we are choosing to miss out on the inheritance we have as sharers of the glory of God.

In one of His conversations with God the Father, Jesus says 'The glory that you have given me I have given to them, that they may be one, even as we are one' (John 17:22). The ability for us to share in the glory of God is ordained by Jesus Christ himself, who is the hope of glory, and it is possible because He lives in us. We also see that there is a purpose to the sharing of His glory and that purpose is to move us towards unity, because, as Jesus says to His followers, 'By this all people will know that you are my disciples, if you have love for one another' (John 13:35). God's glory in seen most in our unity and in how we reflect His love to one another as we are made in the image of the God who is himself love.

Glory in Worship

In my time as a Christian, I have seen God do some pretty amazing things that, for me, have given me small glimpses of His glory. Responses of people in worship, healings, miracles, lives transformed, miraculous provision and people finding freedom in the Spirit, to name a few. There have also been times that the presence of God's glory has caused some things that I haven't fully understood or been able to fully explain. This has been true in my own personal experiences of God too. What I have noticed is that although there have been things that I perhaps haven't had the maturity to understand at the time, the experience of them has not turned me away from God. I have known others who have seen things happen and, because they couldn't explain or understand them, it has made them suspicious of God's Spirit, God's glory and even of God's character as a father. This reminds us that the glory of God is still one of those holy mysteries and it is one that we shouldn't take lightly.

I remember hearing a talk by a church leader a number of years ago. He said that he used to pray, 'Show us your glory, Lord,' each week in their Sunday worship. He did this every Sunday for a number of years, until one day whilst he was praying his usual prayer he heard God say, 'I don't think you would really want me to do that.' In that moment he had a sense that every time he had prayed that prayer, it was as if God had been thinking, 'Really? Is that really what you want? Have you seen what tends to happen when my glory is released and revealed?' In that moment, this Church leader became aware that if God was to come in glory in answer to his prayer then half of his church would have left with suspicion, confusion, or maybe even doubts and fears about God. He realised that the people in his church were not ready to see God's glory, as they lacked the maturity and understanding of God and His glory that was needed to fully appreciate that glory. His prayer from that day changed to,

'God make your people ready for when your glory comes.' God was ready and able to answer that prayer. Over time and through teaching in the church, they began to see glimpses of God's glory as He revealed these signs in His perfect timing. As God revealed His glory, He received the glory for what was happening. Lives were changed because they were open to God's glory – whatever that was going to bring.

Although Jesus has given us a share in God's glory, and although His glory can be experienced by us, we still need to be aware that His glory is sacred, holy and precious, and not to be taken lightly or for granted. If we ever make His glory about us, then God's purpose for sharing that glory is not fulfilled. Yes, God is changing us from glory to glory so that we can be better versions of ourselves, but the ultimate reason for that is so that the glory goes back to Him in our worship of Him. The glory is not ours to own. We only get to share in His, but there is still no greater honour and privilege than that! Are you ready? Would you be open to whatever God wanted to do? Preparedness lies in knowing the goodness of God. The more we know and believe that God is good, the more we can trust that whatever happens when we see His glory will be good, because He is good.

Future Glory

What we experience on earth can only ever be a glimpse of the glory yet to come. During some times of worship there can a be sense that people don't want it to end. Times when we 'finish' the service or prayer meeting and no-one moves and no-one seems to want to leave. These can be a foretaste of the glory to come. It is a glimpse of how glorious eternal worship will be when we have fully surrendered to and are surrounded by God's glory.

Consider those times when you have seen lives transformed through the gospel, or you have heard testimonies of huge transformation taking place in somebody's life and you can sense God getting glory through the words being spoken. Or those stories where the Church is making a huge difference in alleviating suffering around the world; you see people who love Jesus reflecting His glory through how they love and serve the needs of others. Or you see His faithful provision occur in ways that can only lead to Him having the glory – these can be a foretaste of the glory to come.

However, if these are only glimpses of what eternity will be like then just try to imagine what it will be like when we will be with Jesus and will be like Him (1 John 3:2). When we see Him as He truly is, where we can bask in His glory day and night without fear of death. This is an exciting future that lies ahead of us, a future glory that will make everything we face in this life seem rather small. This doesn't undermine our suffering or our joys but it fixes our eyes on the eternal, on the unseen, and becomes the bedrock of our hope. A hope for a greater glory.

It is this image that enables Paul to say what he says in this verse of Romans. In knowledge of our salvation and the privileges and opportunities that come with that salvation, we can look towards a greater glory. It does not mean that suffering is no longer a problem, or that we ignore our pain. Paul is writing to a persecuted church and he is certainly not wanting to play down their struggles. What he is saying is that he personally cannot think of anything that will compare to what is to come. He is essentially saying, 'Hey guys, I get it, persecution is terrible, I've been on both sides of it, and I face persecution now and I know it hurts – but just think for a moment about what is waiting for us. All this suffering will have been more than worth it when God fully reveals His glory to us and we can remain in it.' We can all think of countless analogies of things we have had to endure in order to get something good – queues for a ride, waiting for a delivery, pregnancy before birth – but all of these fall a long way short of what Paul is revealing to the church here. There is no comparison to what is to come for us when we will be with Jesus for eternity. All our present sufferings need to be held up against this hope, this reality to come, this future glory – one yet to be fully revealed to us. Enjoy the glimpses and hold on to them in the difficult times. Greater things are yet to come.

Lord, make me ready for your glory, show me glimpses of your glory, may I share in your glory and may you be glorified in me. Amen!

3 WEAKNESS

the Spirit helps us in our weakness.

-8:26-

I have always loved the idea of being good at art, but unfortunately it has never been more than an idea – I am terrible at drawing, painting, sketching or any similar artistic activities. Our kids will often ask me to draw something for them and then often wonder how what I have drawn is supposed to be what they asked for. If they ask for their faces to be painted I can just about manage a tiger. This is a weakness of mine that I would really like to be a strength, a strength that I admire (and envy) in others. Despite having some guidance when I was younger, and despite using some 'teach yourself to draw' books, this particular art medium is one that I believe will always be a weakness. I have had glimpses in the past of producing a piece of work that I come close to feeling proud of, but I don't think anything I have ever drawn has been seen by anyone else and certainly wouldn't be on display.

Hands up if you think you have it all together, if you have got life sorted and obtained perfection and have no weaknesses? I would hope that no-one has been misguided enough to raise their hands, but if your hands are firmly down then take heart, you are not alone. We all have our own personal strengths of course, which is wonderful and to be celebrated, but we would be kidding ourselves if we believed that there was no weakness within us. We all have weaknesses. I have just given a trivial example of being terrible at art, but I have more life-changing weaknesses than that, some of which can have a massive impact on my life and can stunt my ministry and calling at times. Thankfully, the Bible is full of stories of people who are weak, broken and nothing without God. Despite the world encouraging us to hide our weaknesses, and to be ashamed of them, we find that when we are truly vulnerable we can know and name the weaknesses in us, and the sooner we embrace them and admit them the better it will be for us. This is a sign of strength not weakness.

I don't think that Paul is talking about an inability to do things (like art). He is not talking about strengths and weaknesses in the way that we would on an application form for a job. He is talking here about those areas of weakness that are to do with our character. Those weaknesses in our lives that hold us back from being the people that God has called and purposed us to be. Those weaknesses that slightly mar our reflection of Christ to the world. Those areas in our life where we really need God to work in us, and through us.

Paul appears to be pretty good at embracing his weaknesses. He appears to be very aware of what they are and is able to testify to them and to God's work in spite of them, and often in and through them. If anything, it seems to me that Paul was far more aware of the dangers of his strengths than he was about his weakness. In fact, it could well be that Paul's strengths had the potential to be a trigger for what may have been his greatest weakness.

Pride

In his letter to the Church in Corinth, Paul describes a thorn in his flesh: 'though if I should wish to boast, I would not be a fool, for I would be speaking the truth; but I refrain from it, so that no one may think more of me than he sees in me or hears from me. So to keep me from becoming conceited because of the surpassing greatness of the revelations, a thorn was given me in the flesh, a messenger of Satan to harass me, to keep me from becoming conceited' (2 Corinthians 12:6-7). There are so many speculations in commentaries as to what Paul's thorn in the flesh was. Some say that it was the blindness that he developed later in life, others say his age, others suggest his past, or his current persecution. Often when Paul refers to flesh, he is not just referring to the physical flesh, but also to the part of us that is human, i.e. the fallen, broken, natural state of us. He knows he has been changed by Christ, that his life has been transformed, but he is also aware that he is still a fleshly being, and there are times that his flesh, his humanness, will fight for his attention again. Personally, I believe that this thorn of the flesh was a thorn in his very human nature – could it have been pride?

When you look at the life of Paul it is easy to see why he would have every reason to be a person of pride. As a Jew, he was zealous and devout. As a tent maker, he must have been successful enough to fund his persecution travels. As a persecutor of Christians, he was renowned and very committed to what he did. Then when he encountered Jesus he became a travelling preacher with a hugely successful ministry of church planting, and soon became someone that many people looked up to and whose opinion was greatly valued. He was a great disciple maker and teacher, and he raised up other leaders well. He was passionate and fearless in the face of persecution and he was a visionary with the gospel and a pioneer in sharing it with others. Pride would perhaps, therefore, have played a role in Paul's life. Even if this isn't the thorn in the flesh he refers to, it may well have been something that he battled with.

If I am being honest, I have to say that I certainly hope that this is the case, as it would make me feel a great deal better about my own issues with pride. To know that Paul suffered with this would really help me. To know that God can still work through people the way that he worked through Paul, even if pride is a thorn. Over the years I have had to learn to manage pride. I can't seem to find a way to 'get rid of it' but I am learning ways to cope with it, to be aware of it, to give it its rightful place in my life and to be accountable to others. This particular weakness does not come to the fore when things are hard and when I am struggling, this is a weakness I find to be most prominent when I am strong, when things are going well (at least in human terms). That is when this weakness is vying for my attention, and I will often struggle most with fighting it at these times. Pride isn't always a negative thing. We can take pride in our children, or pride in an accomplishment, but when pride becomes a character trait, that is when we need to see it for what it is.

The reality is, however, that pride is a weakness that we have all suffered from at some point because it is the very root of the sin that separated us from God in the first place. Pride is the root that says: 'I can do it my way.' It's the root that says: 'This will be okay,' when we probably know it really isn't good for us. It's the root that says: 'I don't need God.' The root that says: 'I need attention, look at me.' The root that says; 'I can do this on my own.' The root that says: 'I have a right to blame God when things are not going the way I want them to.' It's the root that declares: 'I am free to live my life how I like.' Pride is the root behind it all – the root behind being driven by a career, money, sex, addiction, or really anything other than a relationship with God. Every human in history has struggled with pride.

True Humility

Paul makes it clear in this verse that when it comes to combatting pride, or any other weakness, there is only one true solution. That one solution is full reliance on the Holy Spirit, which ultimately requires a surrendering and laying down of self. This is the heart of humility. There is a danger, however, when looking at the concept of 'laying down ourselves.' That danger is the ever-present risk of false humility. A. W. Tozer writes that; 'True humility is a healthy thing. The humble man accepts the truth about himself. He believes that in his fallen nature dwells no good thing, he acknowledges that apart from God he is nothing, has nothing, knows nothing and can do nothing. But this knowledge does not discourage him, for he knows also that in Christ he is somebody.'[6] False humility often takes hold of the truth that humility is a healthy thing, taking the first part of a quote like this and accepting it as truth but can often fail to recognise that humility doesn't mean we can't celebrate who we are in Christ. Christ is in us. We cannot, therefore, say that we are completely nothing as that diminishes the reality of us being a new creation in Christ. It can undermine the truth that His spirit is in us, changing us from glory to glory. It is the difference between seeing humility as a 'woe is me' to seeing that we can have humility whilst still saying, 'great is He who lives in me.'

If false humility is the 'woe is me' mentality, what then is true humility? The best definition I have come across is that humility is not thinking less of yourself, but it is thinking about yourself less. This means that you can acknowledge the things you are able to do with Christ, you and others can celebrate those things without it feeding your ego, we can receive compliments and words of encouragement from others, and we are able to, as Charles Spurgeon used to say 'accept the compliment but pass the glory on'. At a time when pride was my greatest enemy, I used to preach or lead worship and then do all I could to avoid people. I would try to look really busy or attempt to make a very quick exit. I feared that compliments would feed my pride monster and the humblest thing to do was to avoid those compliments. I, however, realised one day that this prevented the encouragers in the congregation to do what they are gifted to do. I was not able to grow as a preacher or worship leader because I rarely allowed myself to receive feedback (positive or negative). I knew then that something needed to change in me to allow those things to happen in such a way that it pointed to God and not to me. The focus had to move away from myself and what I got from doing the things I was doing. Looking back now, I can see that I often did things to benefit me, when my focus shifted to serving rather than self-serving, so did my attitude to feedback. Rather than wanting to know if I had 'done a good job', I was keen to know if the sermon had an impact on people's lives, if it had led to any transformation or at least a desire for change. I couldn't know that by hiding. I needed and wanted to hear from the people I was serving. I wasn't reliant on that feedback, as I would always seek God's approval first, but I grew and developed as a preacher when I got it.

Our focus should primarily be on God, then on other people, before it is on us. We need to care for ourselves and look after ourselves, but our motivation comes from our relationship with God first and foremost. It should then be that a desire to serve others becomes a natural outflow of that relationship, and we should realise that caring for ourselves enables us to do this more effectively. This is important because the dangerous alternative is to be so frightened of pride that we become self-deprecating and may even count ourselves out of the idea of God being able to use our gifts and skills, experience, or even our characters, in any way at all. In essence, we may be subconsciously saying, 'God you must have got it wrong, you couldn't possibly want to use me.' People in scripture have said those words for all kinds of reasons – fear, unworthiness, doubt and anxiety – but we must never let a fear of pride stop us from being all that God has called us to be.

Our strengths *and* our weaknesses can be used by God when fully surrendered to Him and they can be tools of humility when we are thinking of others more than we are thinking about ourselves. This is what we see in Jesus; He lives so much for others that there is simply no room for pride in His life. He is the very definition of true humility, the one 'who came not to be served but to serve' (Matthew 20:28), the one who knew utter dependence on the Father (John 5:19) and the one who relied upon the Spirit's leading (Matthew 4:1).

If the Holy Spirit is the Spirit of Christ, then it stands to reason that He is the Spirit of humility too, that humility is one of His key attributes. This means that when we come to a place of full surrender to the Spirit, of reliance on Him, and our need of Him, that can naturally open the door to true humility, which is ultimately total reliance upon God – the very opposite of weakness. Society can often say that humility is a weakness; the Kingdom of God says otherwise.

The Holy Spirit is able to help us in all our areas of weakness, whatever they may be. One glance at the fruits of the Spirit in Galatians 5 of love, joy, peace, patience, kindness, gentleness and self-control, shows us the outworking of having the Spirit in our lives. The description of the love of God in 1 Corinthians 13 does the same. These things become, more and more, symptoms of having the Holy Spirit in us. I remember sharing my personal struggles with my own pride with a prayer triplet I was once part of. One of them said to me that if I was so concerned about being proud then my desire was for humility. If pride was a current and present issue then I would be enjoying it, not wanting to do anything about it – so some of the change must have already taken place, my flesh was just taking a while to catch on to that new reality. The more we allow the Spirit to reign in our lives, the more we allow Him to possess us, the less room there is for pride, or for any of our human failings and weakness that can get in the way. As Christ is seen more in us, as our flesh becomes more in line with His Spirit, the more His 'power is made perfect in [our] weakness' (2 Corinthians 12:9).

If you are someone who suffers from a weak back then you will know that if you take some kind of anti-inflammatory drug it will ease the pain and may well reduce some swelling, but it will not suddenly make your back super strong – the underlying weakness will still be there. When we have Christ in us, when we are fully reliant on His Spirit, then His strength doesn't merely mask our weakness, it works through it and with it. If we are not careful, this can become so normal that we drop back on our reliance on God. When things start to go well, we can forget that we are doing it in His strength, not our own, and can begin to try and take back a little control. The flesh is still part of us and will always be wanting the control – but the difference now is that the Spirit connection with God is there, and through that, God now has the power to win that battle when the will is fully surrendered to the person of the Holy Spirit. Surrender then, needs to be a daily, and at times, hourly thing. When Paul speaks of being filled with the Spirit (see Ephesians 5:18), the translation shows this as an active thing. It is not a case of 'be filled once and the rest of your life will be sorted'. It is better translated as 'be filled and go on being filled'. It is a daily conscious choice to surrender, to rely upon God and to be filled with His Spirit. He can not only help us in our weakness, but can work through it, and do so all the more when we humbly think of ourselves less and of Him and others more.

Lord, I acknowledge my weaknesses, but thank you that your strength can be made perfect through them. Help me to put you and others before myself, and to use what you have given me, through the good and bad experiences of life, to bless those around me and to share your love with others. Amen!

4 PATIENCE

But if we hope for what we do not see, we wait for it with patience.

-8:25-

I am not a very patient person, in fact, I'm often catching myself saying phrases like 'come on, we need to go now!' to our four children as I try to usher them out the door in the morning. I'd like to be able to say that I am just keen to make sure that they are always on time for school (which is partly true). The reality is that I am more concerned about the knock-on effect to the next task that I need to complete that results from them being late, and so in those moments I display impatience.

I'm also not very good at waiting for things. If I know something good is coming, or if something exciting is going to happen, I find it hard to wait. This can often mean that I am terrible at keeping surprises from my wife because if I have secretly booked something fun, I can't wait for her to know. I have this beautiful picture in my mind of her not finding out until the day or time of the surprise. In reality I think I have only achieved this a small handful of times because my own excitement and impatience frequently get the better of me.

This impatience also rears its ugly head in my daily discipleship. If I've prayed and perhaps asked God for clarity on something, it won't be long before my impatience causes me to take matters into my own hands, to attempt to force God's hand, or to try to get a result quicker than He may be planning to give it. I have never noticed this more than when I was applying for a ministry post.

As we approached the end of curacy, I had been asked in late spring to consider applying for an upcoming post. We arranged a meeting straight away with the person who suggested it, to discuss the possibility, and almost instantly, Linz and I felt good about the prospect – could this be God's call? Could we have found our future post? We (very) quickly arranged to visit one of the churches in late July, which we did, and followed that by another conversation with some key people, and we began to get more excited and felt more and more sure of God's call.

We made a beautiful plan in our minds, a plan that would work perfectly. The plan was to have an interview in the middle of August, then we could (if it all still seemed like God's will) accept the offer straight away, move house at the end of August and our children would be able to start in their new school in September. This was a neat and perfect plan – until we heard these words one spring morning: "We need to sort a few things out this end, and there is a delay in putting the profile together, plus there is a lot of work that needs to be done to the house, so the earliest we will be ready to do an interview will be early October." Time seemed to stop. We still felt this was what we should be pursuing but I remember thinking 'Oh great, another lesson in patience.'

If it was another lesson in patience, then I failed – big time! I sent regular emails and made frequent phone calls to ask how the process was going, in the hope that they might say that things were moving quicker than expected. I asked God (a lot) if things could move forward quicker. However, no, we had to wait for what felt like the slowest summer ever, until finally it did all work out in, what I now realise, was God's perfect timing. We were offered the post in October, and due to the proximity with where we were already living, when a space became available in the primary school for our eldest daughter, we were able to take it and commute her to and from school from the October half term. We ended up moving in December. Any earlier and we would not have got our second child into the oversubscribed school, but on the last day of term someone left and so we had a guaranteed space from January. Then after just six weeks of having to home school, our third child got a space too. The reality is that had we moved in September, as per *our* plan, then none of those places would have been available to us. We arrived into the new ministry feeling rested, having had Christmas off for the first time in many years, and it all worked out far better than *we* could have ever planned it to.

I look now at that timescale and in the grand scheme of things, we only had to wait ten weeks longer than we had hoped, so you would be forgiven for thinking that I am quite impatient. There are also, however, things that I have been praying and waiting for, for years, and am still waiting to see the fruit of my labour or the answers to those prayers. Waiting is hard! It is particularly hard, I find, with regard to the people for whom I have been praying for years, desperately asking for them to know Jesus, or to be set free from something that is holding them captive. What I have learnt though, is that impatience can sometimes be, in my life at least, a sign of a distrust in God and His plans for me.

Jesus makes is very clear that we are not to worry about what is to come, or any of our tomorrows (Matthew 6:34). The reality is that many, if not all of us, do. One of the reasons we can find waiting so hard is because with that waiting comes a level of uncertainty.

Being in a state of not knowing is a very difficult thing to live with. The impatient amongst us want to know now! Knowing everything, however, would require no need for trust in God at all.

We also need to remember that patience is a fruit of the Spirit. Life in the Spirit has patience as a natural biproduct. I find it hard to wait on God at times of impatience but that is exactly what we need to do. Not to wait on God for something, not to wait on God for the answer or the certainty, but to wait on God for the sake of spending time in His presence, to draw closer to Him. The best way to 'fill our time' when we are waiting is with God, in His presence. I personally find that waiting with others can make waiting a little more bearable – how much more should this be the case with God. It is here that we learn that His presence is far more important than the thing that we are waiting for anyway and that He holds it all together and holds you in the waiting.

Hope in the Waiting

As Paul states in verse 25, it is in the waiting that we can also discover more about hope. We can have the ability to be patient when we know that whatever we are waiting for will be more than worth the wait. Waiting should not just be about sitting and twiddling our thumbs, though many of us can treat it like that. We can be guilty of thinking that waiting is a passive thing but waiting can be an active thing too. I have found in my life at times that when I am really wanting to see God do something, but at the same time am seeking to find Him in the waiting process, I see glimpses of what it is that I am waiting for. It is like God is giving us a foretaste of what is to come. It can be, at times, an opportunity to look actively for opportunities to *be* an answer to our own prayers. If, for example, we are praying for someone to be free of something, we could pray and wait and do nothing, or we could pray then ask God if there is anything we could be doing, no matter how small, to come alongside that person and help them on their journey to that freedom. If we are praying for someone to come to faith, could we be asking God for opportunities to lead others to faith. This can help to raise our trust and faith in the gospel and its power. Sometimes the process of waiting can be just as, if not more, important than the end result of that waiting, at least for our own growth and development.

One of the ways which I see most often as a pitfall of pacifism, or expecting God to do our work for us, is when I come across people praying for revival. I believe that we should pray for revival and that many revivals in history began with prayer and a desire for holiness. But these moves of God also happened in places where people were already deeply involved in social justice and where the church was working towards changing the society around them. The revival had already happened in the church and its people were wanting to do all they could for the people around them. When the prayers of the saints met with the mission of the church, God did things that only God can do. I have been involved in prayer movements in the past where people are praying and praying for revival, but it feels a bit like they want revival because it would be far easier for them if God did all the work. But we are called to pray and to serve. The commission was given to us by God; He promised that He will build His church, but also desires to work with and through her. There are times that God does step in and do incredible miracles and times when He saves entire towns, villages and even countries, but the question is: if you are praying for, hoping for, and waiting for revival, what can you be doing in the waiting to be the hands and feet of Jesus? I don't mean striving, or doing everything, but I am talking about asking God where He may be calling us to be the answer to our own prayers in the waiting. Where we can be the hope. I believe this shows we have a hope that is not only worth praying for and waiting for, but that is also worth living for and sharing with the world. This does not make us seem impatient because there are things we do need to wait for, and the waiting is a good thing, but we have an opportunity to grow in our relationship with God, and to develop our hope in Him during that patient waiting.

I believe, however, that some things are never intended to be fruitful until much later in our lives. If you think of gardening as an analogy, you sow in one season, but the fruit is rarely produced in the same season. We often have to wait for at least the next season. When we moved into our most recent house, we removed some unwanted bushes from our garden. In the spring, we sowed some grass seed where the bush had been. I (impatiently) checked every day to see if the seed had worked. For the first few days there was nothing, not even a hint of grass (despite the promises on the packet). A few days later we began to see the odd shoot of grass. After a couple of weeks, the grass had grown but was still really patchy. Eventually, by the end of the summer we were mowing that bit of grass. Even then, the growing process still hadn't finished. The following spring when we came to do the first mow of the year, the whole area that we had cleared was massively overgrown, with the new grass, with self-seeded grass from elsewhere in the garden and even with grass that was probably under the bush before we dug it out. It had taken a whole year of seasons for what we had sown, and even what others may have sown, for the grass patch to fully come to harvest.

The same can be true for us spiritually; that what we sow (in prayer or in mission) can take time to harvest. In some cases, if it was to harvest too soon it may not be as fruitful or as bountiful as it could be if given more time. Paul speaks specifically of the importance of time and patience when sowing in Galatians 6:8-9: 'For the one who sows to his own flesh will from the flesh reap corruption, but the one who sows to the Spirit will from the Spirit reap eternal life. And let us not grow weary of doing good, for in due season we will reap, if we do not give up.'

When we are sowing things of the Spirit, we also need to trust the Spirit with the timing and the end result of the harvest. Only He knows the best, true and proper time, or even if the harvest is in His plan at all. In the waiting we do what we are responsible for doing – continuing to do good, and not tiring to do so (Galatians 6:9). This is the antidote to the potential of becoming resentful for not getting what we want, when we want it.

It is important to find a balance, however, between patiently waiting and actively seeking. Ironically this particular fruit of the Spirit requires us to be willing to wait in God's presence in order to receive it. To lay the things that we are waiting for, and that are important to us, before God. Patience, like all the fruits, is not a fruit of human striving but a fruit of the Spirit in us. I often find that when my fuse is short with my kids it is a symptom of impatience in my life and I know I need to rest in God and allow him to grow that fuse – He always does a far better job than when I try to do that myself. Whilst I would love to just be a patient person NOW, the reality is that if I was, I would depend less on God in times of waiting, and could miss out on a part of God's love or desires for me in that time.

What are we Waiting for?

The 'waiting' that Paul is referring to in Romans 8, is the waiting for what is to come; that of the future glory he mentions a few verses before. For the Christian, what we are waiting for has the guarantee of being worth the wait. Patience for us is a matter of trusting who holds the future, and the goodness of His nature and His promises – which makes us certain of the goodness of that future.

Keeping our eyes on this truth is important because it helps us with understanding our need for surrender. When we surrender our plans to God we need to be willing to surrender all our plans to God, even the ones we think we have 'sorted'. Let's face it, we probably all have things for which we have been praying for many years, but have not yet seen the answer to. We can easily feel disappointed, ignored, let down, and can even blame God for the lack of answer. Real patience doesn't only trust God with the timing, it also trusts God with the end result, even if that turns out to be a million miles from what we would have wanted or hoped for. This is why it is so important to remember that in the waiting, God knows what He is doing, He is in control, He has an eternal picture, of which we do not yet have full insight.

Patience requires trust, and it is helped along by hope. Before verse 25, Paul has set up the context of our hope and the character of the God we hope and trust in. He has given us an eternal perspective on all the other things we are waiting for. We can wait for this patiently, but we don't have to wait statically. Our hope is sure and certain, but while we wait for it, there is an even higher call. We are reminded in Corinthians that as important as faith and hope are, as things that will always remain, there is one thing greater than these and that is love (see 1 Corinthians 13:13). If we are waiting impatiently, we may be missing opportunities to love others, and in that love to share the hope that we have. There are some (many) things about God we will never fully understand. There are questions to which we may never know the answers. There may be answers to prayer that are not the ones we were hoping for. There are fruits to our prayers that we may not see in our lifetime. The question is: will any of these things cause you to love God any less?

Patience can be really hard. Although it is a fruit of the Spirit, there are times it can be painful, surprising and even, at times, life altering – but in the waiting, let us never miss the opportunities to love, to share hope, to be the answer to our own prayers and the prayers of others. Let us never pin our love of God on the answers to our prayers but remember that He is not only at the destination but is also with us in the waiting.

Lord, in times I am impatient will you help me to trust you. For the things I am waiting for, will you grant me glimpses of the hope that is to come. Where I am hoping for things that are not in your plans for me, help me to trust you more. In the waiting, help me to prioritise my time with you, to grow closer to you in the process and keep my eyes on what you have promised to those who love you. Amen!

5 SET YOUR MIND

For those who live according to the Spirit, set their minds on things of the Spirit.

-8:5-

There is a common misconception by those who have never done tightrope walking before, that the best thing to fix your gaze on is your feet. When I was at college I was involved in a school production of *Barnum* (a musical based around the life of P.T. Barnum). The show has many circus skills involved within the production. I mainly had to learn to juggle and sing at the same time, but my good friend who was playing Barnum had to learn to walk a tight rope (albeit one very close to the ground). As I was his understudy for the show, I also had to learn this particular skill, just in case it went very wrong for the lead actor! After many failed attempts, the person teaching us said, "Don't look at your feet, you feel with your feet, but you look at where you are heading -- to the end point." So, we fixed our gaze on the end platform, and after a few more practices we managed it. (Thankfully all went well, and I just had to stick to my new-found juggling skill and never had the need to tightrope walk again.)

Fixing our eyes on a particular goal is a common theme for Paul. He talks elsewhere about running the race and keeping our eyes on the end goal, the goal which is ultimately Jesus (Acts 20:23-24). To the church in Rome, however, he is talking about fixing minds on things of the Spirit – not just our gaze or our focus, but our logic, our thinking, our learning, our wills, our thoughts, fixing on the end goal rather than our feet.

Setting your Mind

As Paul moves his focus on the flesh, in the previous verse, onto the mind in this verse, he is showing that there is a stark contrast between the two. This is significant because Paul is seeking to show the Roman Christians, and the church as a whole, that we are holistic people, made of body, mind and spirit, and that the truth of the gospel has the power to transform us entirely, each and every part of us.

Our minds are an important part of who we are. What we think has tremendous power to impact what we are feeling and ultimately how we then act. When Paul refers to the mind, he is not only referring to our intellect, or our theological thinking; He is referring to the whole mind. He is including intellect and thinking, but there is likely to be a particular emphasis intended on the will of our minds. He is wanting to challenge the readers of this message to make the things of God, and the will of God, their primary thought, and to fix their minds on the one who reveals God's will, the Spirit of Christ.

I have heard it said that what you spend most of your time thinking about when you are left to your own thoughts will show, at least on some level, what is most important to you at that time. If you are always thinking about the person you love, your spouse, your children, then they are important to you. If you are constantly wondering when you will get a chance to watch the next episode of your favourite TV show, then that is important to you. Big things, and trivial things can become important to us. Some remain important to us and others come and go and lose their importance over time. Our hearts naturally respond to what is on our minds, and as Jesus so observantly states, 'where your treasure is, there your heart will be also' (Matthew 6:21).

It is also true of the negative things that we spend our time thinking about, or even worrying about. If you are constantly worried about things that need to be done, then completing tasks may be very important to you. If you are always thinking about what others are thinking about you, then your image is important to you, or perhaps it is important to you that you please others. If you are worried about money, then financial security is important to you…the list of examples goes on. Some of these preoccupations may not seem like negative things in and of themselves, but if they dominate the landscape of our thinking they can become so.

What do you spend most of your time thinking about? When you have moments to yourself, what fills your mind? Pause your reading for a bit. Take a moment to be still and to think. What is coming to your mind first?

Were what came to mind things of the flesh or of the Spirit?

What does it even mean to set our minds on things of the Spirit? Thankfully, Paul does expand on this theme more in Chapter 12 of this letter: 'I appeal to you therefore, brothers, by the mercies of God, to present your bodies as a living sacrifice, holy and acceptable to God, which is your spiritual worship. Do not be conformed to this world, but be transformed by the renewal of your mind, that by testing you may discern what is the will of God, what is good and acceptable and perfect' (12:1-2).

Paul shows that there is a necessity for our minds to be renewed, to be made anew. You will notice that this particular mention of the mind in Romans 12 is in the context of worship. Worship is the act of directing our adoration, praise, thanksgiving and honour. Worship is to give God His worth. Worship is ultimately about what we are setting our mind upon. So, what you are setting our mind upon, as well as being important to you, also has the potential risk of becoming an object of your worship. This is why our minds need to be renewed so that the object of our worship is God and God alone. Our whole lives are to be an offering of worship to our God, so it is not simply a case of setting our minds on God on a Sunday morning, but in all that we do. Renewal of the mind is essential for making this not only possible, but achievable. There are two aspects of the renewal of the mind, two parts to be played – one by us and the other by God.

1. Our Part

There is a large element of the renewal of our minds that is to do with self-control. In other words, we need to ask what we are choosing to fill our minds with. When talking about our children, my Grandma always used to say, "You get out what you put in." That is to say that if you invest in something, if you put in the right things, then you get good things from it. In the context of parenthood, she would have been referring to things like good discipline, quality time, healthy foods and ultimately love. The same can be said of our minds. What you 'feed' your mind with is of huge importance. It can make a massive impact, often unnoticed at first, on what you get from your mind when it is left to wander.

Let me give you an example. An example that may seem extreme, but it is something that affects a huge number of people around the world and fills many people with shame, despite much of society considering it as harmless. This particular activity is something that many people might justify because 'lots of people do it and it's fine'. This is something that is more accessible now than it has ever been and the average age that people are introduced to it now is 11 years old. I am referring to pornography. You may not have expected this to be a topic covered in this book, but it is a helpful example of the important need for renewal of the mind.

For years people have thought that despite it being degrading and not good for people under the age of 18, pornography is largely considered to be harmless. Recent studies have shown, however, that this is simply not true. Engaging with pornography has proven to have devastating effects on relationships, mental health and peace of mind for so many people. The invaluable work of the Naked Truth Project and similar organisations are now shining a light on the damage that pornography causes and is making people aware of the long-term effects that it can have. The issue of shame being one of the most damaging outcomes.

The images that we feed into our minds, even from years ago, can have a habit of sticking around for a very long time, and can re-emerge when we least expect them to. For the couple who have one of the partners living with a pornography addiction, there can be major implications on intimacy, as thoughts and images that the mind has been fed with, create an unrealistic expectation of what sex should look like, feel like and be like. This, in turn, can rob the couple of the joy of mutually satisfying love making. All of this, and more, can come from a mind that has been poorly fed in the past (or maybe for some still in the present), due to an addiction to pornography. Even if it is not being currently fed now, or rather is being fed the wrong things, renewal is still very much needed, and thankfully is possible, so there is hope.

I know this is a strong example, but it is also an extremely common one, and is something that so many people struggle with (and not just men, women can have porn addictions too). Whether pornography is an issue for you or not, the reality is that whatever we feed our minds can have a lasting effect. The same can be true of violent games, films or graphic novels, to name a few examples. I am not talking here about having complete abstinence from films, TV or gaming. I am simply highlighting some of the possible causes of what would be considered as a badly fed mind. It is about knowing your own limits and knowing what affects you, knowing what images and thoughts prove difficult for you to get rid of. I remember once watching a TV show that had one very violent scene in it. In the past these things have not really bothered me. I have been able to switch off the TV at the end of the show, forget the violent bits and just carry on. This particular scene stayed with me. The following Sunday I was in church and someone was leading the intercessions, and with my eyes closed all I could picture was this scene, playing over and over again in my mind. I became aware of the preoccupation of it and knew I needed God's help to renew that mind, but I also made a conscious decision to not watch the rest of that particular TV series, aware that it was having a negative impact on my mind.

Let us look for a moment at the alternative that Paul presents to us in Romans 8 – setting your mind on the things of the Spirit. The more we read of God's word, for example, the more of His word we remember. The more we listen to worship music, the more positive thoughts about Jesus will be bounding around our heads when 'that song' gets stuck and won't get out. The more we engage with our brothers and sisters in Christ, the more we may be thinking about the things we talk about and share between us in our meeting together. The more we spend time making ourselves aware of the reality of being in a broken world, the more our thoughts will be turned towards justice and those situations in need of our intercession. The more we think about the love of God, the more aware our minds will become of those in need of that love. The more we think about what God has done in our lives (perhaps by journaling and reading back over those entries) the more easily we are able to trust God's faithfulness when harder times come. Ultimately, the more our minds are being grateful and thankful, the better the attitude we have towards the life God has given us.

We have a responsibility to do these things intentionally, to choose to do them, to choose to learn the difference between right and wrong, to know what helps us, feeds us, encourages us closer to God, to turn our mind to things of the Spirit and to fix it there. God will not love us any less if we fail to do so, but we will find that it is easier to have the 'mind of Christ' (1 Corinthians 2:16), if we fix our minds on things of the Spirit.

2. God's Part

A few years ago, at a Christian event, a friend of mine, Simon (not his real name), was stood in the main worship session. There came a time after the talk, when the person on stage encouraged the people gathered to wait on the Spirit. The band gently played in the background and after a few moments, things began to happen, for everyone, it seemed, except Simon. He waited patiently for his moment, for his bolt of electricity, for his tears, his laughter, for his voice to cry out in tongues (as per Acts 2:4, or Mark 16:17), but nothing, absolutely nothing. The leader on stage began to speak out some of the things that he sensed were happening. "Some of you may be feeling a warm sensation" – not Simon! "Some of you may be crying, or weeping, or even laughing" – not Simon! "Some of you may be having an increased desire of boldness for evangelism or justice" – not Simon! The list continued to grow and still 'nothing' was happening for Simon. That was until the leader on stage said, "Some of you may be receiving a sharpening or a renewal of your mind." Then it happened. Without asking for it, without having even thought about it through the hour of worship and a talk, Simon received absolute clarity on a decision he had been struggling with for weeks. He had prayed about it, he had sought the advice and guidance of others, he had written down all the pros and cons, but he had just not been able to work out the right way forward. In that moment, in that tent, as he waited on the Spirit (expecting the kind of things that were happening to others around him), he actually experienced a clarity of mind like he had never experienced before. In that moment, the Spirit of God was renewing his mind.

As well as there being a responsibility on our part, sometimes there is some work that needs to be done in our minds that only God can do. What we need to do is give Him the opportunity to do it and trust Him for the rest. Simon could have walked away when 'nothing was happening' for him, but he made a conscious decision to stay, to give God time, to keep trusting that God would do something. He remained; God renewed. This was also a culmination of all the seeking after God's will that Simon had been choosing to do leading up to this event. When Simon had done all that he could do, God stepped in and showed what He could do.

Far too often in our times of worship, or prayer, we can rush away before waiting to see if there is something God wants to do with our minds. We may present our requests to God and then get on with our day, when perhaps what we need is to wait a little longer for what God wants to do. He may have some form of renewal He wants to bring to our minds. We may even do a bit of waiting, and maybe once we have had the 'emotional feeling', we might think that God has finished with us. However, He may still have some work to do in our minds. He could be wanting to bring the kind of renewal that would be an answer to our prayers in a different way from that which we might expect. He could be wanting to change our perspective on what we are praying for.

Imagine a person who has a long-term illness. Every time she prays, she asks God to take the sickness away, to bring the healing that she desperately wants and needs. God can totally do those things, so it is good to ask Him for them, but what if the sickness remains? What if it isn't taken away? What if years of asking brings no change to her circumstances? Her life may become defined by the illness, everything may revolve around it, there is potential for her life to be governed entirely by it. God may well get full blame and possibly even be completely rejected as a result of 'unanswered prayer'.

Now let's imagine this same person, who has been diagnosed with the same terminal illness. She sits down with God, cries out to Him, tells Him how she feels, she asks for the illness to be taken away and for healing to come. Then she waits. She simply waits for the Holy Spirit to speak. As she waits she doesn't *feel* anything, healing from the illness does not come, and although she still believes that God can and does heal, what she finds is that gently, slowly, somehow her perspective is changing. She finds herself beginning (only beginning but that's enough for now) to accept the illness she has for now, begins to accept that although God can change things, for some reason right now this illness is something that is her reality. Not in a way that causes her to give up seeking healing, or that stops her from hoping. She's not going to stop praying for healing, but she also refuses to be defined by that illness *if* the healing does not come. She knows, somehow, she *knows* even though she can't feel it, she knows that God is with her in this. She is reminded of His faithfulness to her in the past. Verses that she had committed to memory about God's goodness and kindness come flooding back into her mind. She is experiencing a peace that is beyond all human understanding (Philippians 4:7), and it is not a feeling, it's an awareness that God is with her. It is a peace that is not reliant on the circumstances around her being right, but that comes from a secure knowledge of who Jesus is. She doesn't need the feelings, she may long for them still and they may still serve her well at other times, but right now the feelings would only enhance what she *knows*. She *knows* she is God's daughter. She *knows* that she is loved. She *knows* that He is with her. She *knows* that her Father in heaven cares. She *knows* that He will give her what she needs each day, even each moment. She is still, and she knows that He is God!

There is a well-known psalm about this, which doesn't call us to be still and feel that He is God. The call is to 'be still and to *know* that He is God' (Psalm 46:10). You may have seen from the above example how the two aspects of God's part and our part work together in the renewal of our minds. The lady with the illness had previously filled her mind with things of the Spirit. When things were good and the circumstances were good, she had made the decision to read, pray, seek fellowship and worship. Then, when she needed them most, and when she waited on Him, God, by His renewing Spirit, bought those memories of His goodness to the foreground. As she gave Him time to do so, He renewed her mind, changed her perspective, reminded her of truth, secured her identity in Him and, even though the illness was still a reality, on a level far deeper than physical or even emotional, He healed her in the process.

Knowing you are His

In my own life, when I have given God time to renew my mind when facing a challenge, I have found that one of the key things He does is to remind me who I am in Him. It is amazing what difference it makes to know that we are His. I was recently with someone going through some difficult times. When I asked her how she was, her reply was beautiful: "I am thankful for the steadiness that I have inside". She went on to explain that despite all the storms that were going on around her, she felt spiritually secure, as if there was a steadiness deep within her that provided her with hope, security, stillness and even peace – the peace that Paul describes as passing all human understanding. All this steadiness came from an assurance of who she was in Christ. The circumstances around her could never change or alter that truth.

There is something remarkable, and even life changing, about knowing that we are permanently in the presence of Jesus, and even more so that He is in us. This knowledge can make a huge difference when we face trials in our lives. The story of Jesus calming the storm (Matthew 8:23-27, Mark 4:38-40) reminds us of this. Despite the storm raging, Jesus was able to sleep in peace. He knew where His security was – in the Father. He maybe even knew that death would not be the end of Him. The disciples were focused on the storm so the circumstances (perhaps understandably) overwhelmed them. They were not, in that moment, centred on who was in the boat with them. To cut the disciples some slack, let's not forget this was still a fairly new relationship.

The closer we are to Jesus, or rather the more aware we are of Christ being in us, the more that sense of steadiness is there when the storm comes. In fact, keeping Jesus at the centre, and being fully aware of what that truth does to our identity, can bring an indescribable sense of calm and stillness. In the eye of any major storm there is an area where it is very calm. It seems impossible when you look at a storm to imagine that the safest, or at least the calmest, place to be would be right in the centre, but this is what I imagine is happening spiritually with Jesus in the boat. He is calm in the storm because He is *the* calm in the storm. We can know in our own storms, whatever they may be, that the calm of the storm is in us.

When we know, truly *know*, that our identity is in Christ, that we are children of God, when we know our Heavenly father well, we can be in a storm but still have that steadiness, that peace that passes understanding. This is all to do with the will of the mind being turned to Jesus. It is to do with setting our minds on the things of the Spirit and allowing God to renew our minds by shifting our focus from the situation or circumstances, to the one who has command over even the wind and the waves.

Dear Lord, I entrust to you the circumstances of my life. When the storms rage around me, help me to be secure in who I am in you and in the truth of who you are. Holy Spirit, as I wait upon you now, I ask that you renew any part of my mind that needs renewal, and that through that renewal you will bring the transformation I need. I choose today to set my mind on the things of the Spirit. Amen!

ADOPTED

6 ADOPTION

but you have received the Spirit of adoption

-8:15-

It was just after Easter and I was dropping the children off to school when I saw a dad that I hadn't seen before. I thought that maybe he was new to the area, so I introduced myself and asked if he had recently moved in. I was surprised to discover that he had been in the area for quite some time but that the children he was now dropping to school for the first time had just been adopted by him and his wife. Over the weeks that followed we came to know this family very well, our children had regular play dates together, and the father and I shared a love of films and the occasional game of tennis. He and his kids even introduced our eldest daughter to Star Wars on a sleepover, for which I am truly grateful – she has been a fan ever since.

As we got to know this family more, I was amazed to learn about the adoption process that this family had to endure to give two children a new forever home. It was a long and drawn-out process, which at times came with huge emotional cost. Through it all, what was clear was the love that these two new parents had for the children that they had chosen to bring into their home, and their desire to do their absolute best for those kids.

'Chosen', 'wanted', 'special' – these are just three words that are often used by adoptive parents to describe the children they give a forever home to. I have found that the more I understand about adoption in the human sense, the more significant it becomes to know that we have been adopted by God. It has always been His intention to adopt us, to give us a new forever home. This is beautifully reflected when a family choose adoption on earth.

J. I. Packer states that the concept of adoption is the most important part of the gospel narrative: 'You sum up the whole of the New Testament teaching a single phrase, if you speak of it as a revelation of the Fatherhood of the Holy Creator.'[7] This is why we see so much about adoption in Paul's writing, not only in Romans but elsewhere too. This is why we see gospel writers highlighting the relationship between Jesus and the Father. This is why Paul highlights it in the centre of his main point in this letter defining the gospel to the church in Rome.

You were chosen, and what is more, 'you were bought at a price' (1 Corinthians 6:20). A price that had to be paid to destroy the sin that separated you from a father who loves you, who has chosen you, who wants you, who sees you as special and precious in His eyes. As that price is paid and as you accept what Jesus has done for you, through repentance and admitting your absolute need of Him in your life, you have received 'the right to become children of God' (John 1:12). All adoptions require a legal transaction to take place, and this has happened spiritually for us on the Cross of Jesus Christ. What amazing grace!

Understanding this Spirit of adoption was crucial for Paul, and his desire was that the Christians in Rome really understood what it meant to be adopted by God the Father, and so his use of adoption language was very deliberate and well thought out. Paul would have been writing this to a community of people who were steeped in the gospel stories of Jesus. They would have been gathering regularly to hear these stories, and so it is likely that when Paul talks of God as a father who has adopted us, the hearers would have been able to call to mind the times Jesus spoke of God as *the* Father.

The Prodigal Son

I am a firm believer that it is impossible to write about God's adoption of us without looking at the story of the prodigal son, a narrative of Jesus that so perfectly illustrates the relationship between God and us. It highlights an important point about not only knowing, but also accepting the identity that God has given us as His adopted and chosen children. Although this story is about a biological son, what it reveals to us is the love of the Father that we have been adopted by.

I am sure that this story is so very familiar that it would be tempting to skip over it, or to speed read through it. I want to encourage you, however, to put this book down, pick up your Bible and read through Luke 15:11-32 slowly, reflectively, and as you do, to ask God to give you fresh eyes to see your identity as a son or daughter of God through its familiar words.

I want to focus on three major themes that we can learn by using the three characters. Through a brief reflection we will consider: the identity of the son who returns home, the place in which that identity is found, and the wrong or misplaced sense of identity of the older son.

The Prodigal

It is clear in this story that something in this younger son is dissatisfied with the way things are. He feels an urge or a need to take matters into his own hands, to be the master of his own destiny. He wants to get to decide how he lives his life, spend his time, his money, and his days. There appears to be a 'grass must be greener on the other side' mentality going on in this man's mind. We don't know or find out from the story why this is, and it becomes more confusing when later in the story he looks back with fondness on what he had before. We can probably assume, however, that the driving force is probably the same driving force that is behind all our rebellion. The pride that says, 'I can do it better' or perhaps, 'I'll do it my way.'

The son, then, is seemingly searching for some kind of purpose. He may not know it, be aware of it, or acknowledge it, but he is working out what to do with his life. He has a deep longing to discover his identity and so he goes in search of it. He takes his early inheritance from his father – probably thinking that without money he would have no status in the world, perhaps thinking he doesn't want to work but would rather just enjoy life. The process of taking the money and leaving the family unit likely brings shame on the family name.

We know from the story that he tried to find his identity in all kinds of things. Many commentators and preachers (and I include myself in this, from the times I have told this story to children in various schools) will embellish this part of the story and will speculate as to how he wasted his money and what he spent it on, and what was meant by the term 'squandered'. The reality is that we don't know, and this was a story Jesus was telling, not a real-life event, so He was probably allowing some details to be left to the hearer's imagination. We don't know how long it took him to lose the money, but it is clear to us that there was a drastic change in his circumstances. Some of these circumstances were caused by his own doing: he wasted the money, he chose not to find work earlier, he left home in the first place. Some of the circumstances were out of his control: the famine in the land, the lack of work available when he needed it the most.

This all goes some way to reveal something important about where we find our identity. We can define our identity using all kinds of things in life, and many of these things can appear to be very good – our family, our job, our income, our status in society, our friendships. Ask yourself these very important and difficult questions: 'What if all that were to be stripped away tomorrow? Where would your identity be then?' Many professional sports men and women struggle with losing their sense of identity when they can no longer compete professionally. The majority of sports have a relatively young retirement age. Most footballers, for example, will retire from professional sport before the age of 40. For most of their life (often since a very young age) that sport would have been all that they have known. Unless they end up as a coach, manager or even a pundit, the sport can no longer be the thing that brings them income, identity and status – so the question becomes for them, as for all of us at some stage in life: 'What am I if I am not that?'

The prodigal son felt he didn't need his father and the life he offered any more. Far too many people live this life feeling as though they don't need God, that they can have all they need without him. Their identity can be placed in other things. I have a friend who once said to me, "I've got this far without God and I am doing OK, why would I need Him now?" My challenge to him is to ask, 'have you really got this far without God or simply without the acknowledgement of God?' I wonder if his opinion would change if some of his 'comfort' or 'okayness' were to be suddenly taken away. I'd also like to ask whether just being 'OK' is what we were made to be? The Father offers us so much more than just OK, as we will see later in the story.

The reality is that we all *need* God. I remember talking to somebody in the street about Jesus and she asked me, "Isn't he just a crutch for people?" Well in a way, absolutely He is. He is of course not *just* a crutch – the truth is I do need Him. I would be lost without Him. I can't bear to think about what my life would be like without Him, but I don't see that as a bad thing or a weakness. We spend the younger years of our lives learning to be independent of our parents, but we must never lose our utter dependence upon God as our heavenly Father – a lesson that the prodigal was learning the hard way.

For the son in this story there is a gradual realisation that he needs something, something that he had before but didn't recognise for what it was. Something that no money could buy, something that couldn't be earned, or worked for. He needed a relationship with a father who loves him, and wants what is best for him. A father who is so full of grace that he was willing to let his son go and discover the world, despite the pain it may have caused to let him go. He needed God. I need God. You need God. The person sitting next you on the train needs God. We all need God. No matter how comfortable our life may appear to be, we could only be one financial crash away from losing our job, one accident away from losing a loved one. One pandemic away from losing everything we hold dear. If any of these things are that which we put our identity and purpose in, then we are trusting in things that will pass away. I would rather my identity rest in something eternal, something sure…or rather, some*one* eternal and sure.

The Father

People with no Christian faith would have differing views of what Christians find their identity in. I find it interesting to hear non-Christians describe what they think Christians say about who they are as believers. The truth is that identity, for the Christian, is found in a person not a thing, title, status or background. Society often says things like 'you are what you eat' or 'being from that place means that you must…'. Everywhere we look, people are encouraged to find their identity in stuff, in status, in their looks, in where they come from. This isn't a new problem; it was even said of Jesus, 'can anything good come from [Nazareth]?' (John 1:46). For the Christian, our true identity is found in the Godhead. A perfect heavenly Father, who we can have a relationship with because of the life, death and resurrection of the Son and the Spirit who lives in us. Unlike anything this earthly world can offer you, this is a secure, unfailing, unchanging, unending, reliable, trustworthy, good, holy and righteous place in which to find your identity.

In the story, the father is found waiting. From the moment the son leaves home, he waits. Again, the story is often embellished a bit here. Does the father sit at the window moping around? Does he show signs of depression? Does he spend his days shuffling around in his slippers and dressing gown? Well if this is a picture you have of God the Father then No! God doesn't cease to be a father any less than God would cease to be God when we choose to walk away from Him, to live outside of His love for us. Whilst He may grieve the loss of relationship, He still continues to be active in the world, caring for *all* His children. This father can wait and act simultaneously. He can still be the father to the other son (even though that son may not have seen that). He could still run the family estate, keep things functioning. God, as father, would ultimately know that the son would one day return. This reveals a mind-boggling reality that is also a mystery – God is a father who doesn't need us, but He wants us. He chooses us, longs for us, desires us, and perhaps at times even pursues us. If you go through your whole life choosing not to enjoy the life-changing relationship with this heavenly Father, then it will not make Him any less the God He is now. You will be the one missing out. When you choose to come to Him... just look at the reaction He will give.

As the son wearily arrives home, frightened of what he might find, expectant of the wrath and righteous and justified anger, he finds the father running to greet him, throwing his arms around him and showing him love. The items that the father now gives to the son are symbols of significance, authority, worth, status, and ultimately confirm his identity as his son. Only servants walked barefoot, so the father gave the son sandals. The ring is considered by many commentators to have not been just any ring but in fact the family signet ring, showing that the son has been reinstated to the family and even once again become entitled to an inheritance, despite having already wasted one.

The truth of our adopted status is one of the great mysteries of the gospel that I don't think we will ever fully understand this side of heaven. God doesn't need you. He simply wants you. You are valuable to Him, precious to Him, His prize possession. You are worth everything to Him, even dying for, and He will not let you go and nothing and no one can take you from Him. Christ is now in you, and nothing can change that.

God didn't make us because he was lonely and needed us. He made us, created us in His image, for His pleasure and delight. When we messed up, He went on to save us. All of this was motivated by love. Personally, I think this is far more powerful than *me* being the answer to a 'needy' God's pining wish.

The adoption that God offers to us brings about a significant change to our intimacy with God. Not necessarily about how much God loves us, but rather how He loves us and how He views us as He deals with what prevented us from being able to have intimacy with Him. It is clear throughout scripture that God abhors sin. We, in our natural fallen state, are covered in that sin, even defined by it. As previously explored, the root of that sin is pride and rebellion. It is hard for any parent to have an intimate, affectionate, close and loving relationship with a child who is choosing separation and disobedience. That parent will absolutely love that child and will long for them to 'come back home' but they won't have the same level of intimacy; there is a disconnection, a barrier to the relationship. In our case that barrier is, or was, the sin caused by our disobedience. As we turn to Christ something significant happens. We are made new (2 Corinthians 5:17), we are washed clean, forgiven, restored. Then the ultimate transaction happens as Christ not only forgives us, but clothes us with righteousness (Isaiah 61:10, 2 Corinthians 5:21). More than that however, Christ takes up His dwelling in us (Galatians 2:20). Now, when the Father looks at us, He sees Christ. He views us in the same way that He views His one and only son. When you look at how God speaks of Jesus at his baptism (Matthew 3:13-17) that has to be a different kind of precious.

There are many different opinions on God's view of us pre- and post-adoption. There are those who say that when God looks at us, all He sees is Jesus. There are others who say that when He looks at us, He sees us, with all our human failing and weakness, but thankfully loves and accepts us regardless, *because* of Jesus. Personally, I don't think it is as clear cut as this. I believe this is one of those mysteries that is not an either/or situation but rather a both/and situation. When God looks at you, He sees and loves the unique *you*. He wants relationship with *you*. He loved *you* enough to send His son for *you*! At the same time, however, He sees Christ, His beloved son, and that makes a difference to the view He has of you.

It is the view of Christ in us that means there is no condemnation, and it is the view of us that moves Him to want us to be the best versions of ourselves that we can possibly be.

We are precious enough before adoption for Him to want to save us in the first place, but once that barrier of sin is removed, once we have chosen life with Him, we are adopted into His family and welcomed home with an intimate embrace. In his book *Just Like Jesus,* Max Lucado says: 'God loves us. And not only does God love each of us as we are, he wants us, little by little, to become like him. He doesn't love us and leave us alone; he loves us enough to live within us, making our hearts his home.'[8] From that moment of saying 'yes' to a relationship with Jesus and accepting him into our lives, Jesus becomes 'Christ in us', and He begins to make us more like Him on a daily basis. Obedience then becomes about surrendering to that process knowing that whatever He wants to do in us, it will be for our good and in the process, we are secure in Him. He wants us to become more like His Son in how we live. The primary area of our lives where God longs for us to become more like Jesus is how we relate to Him as our Father – how we know His love for us and how we love Him in return.

A few years ago, I was preaching on this theme and was really struggling to communicate it well. A conversation after the sermon led me to pray and ask God how to communicate the message better at the next service. As I was driving between the two churches the word 'incarnation' came to my mind. It was in that moment I realised I was trying to put words to something that is as profoundly mysterious as the incarnation of Jesus. This is something we will never fully grasp this side of heaven, but we can still accept the truth of it and allow it to transform our lives. If, after reading this, you are still confused about how God views us pre-and post-adoption, then I believe we are in good company! We can be sure, however, that he ultimately views us with the love of a perfect father.

The Older Son

Many preachers I have heard and commentaries I have read have reflected on the second son. Most of the commentaries or reflections that I have read seem to talk about what he shows us about jealousy, pride, envy, anger and our comparison of our faith with that of another. I can see why these conclusions have been reached and they are very true and good lessons to learn from these few verses of the older son's reaction to his brother's return. There is easily more than one way to interpret this part of the parable (as indeed is true of most of Jesus' parables).

Personally, I think there is a deeper issue going on here. The second son appears to have a huge misunderstanding of his own identity. In his anger and disappointment, this older son can't believe that his younger brother gets all the special treatment, especially considering what he has been doing to serve his father the whole time the younger son has been away. No doubt he had to pick up much of the work that the younger brother 'should' have been doing. These feelings are worsened by the elder son's sense of entitlement; he feels he deserves what his younger brother has received. After all, he has worked hard for his father his entire life, he has always served him faithfully, he has always done what was asked of him and even things that have not been asked of him. Unlike his brother, he has never tried to run away or shame his father's name, yet he has never had a feast, he's possibly never been given a robe or a ring. It seems so unjust to him. Ultimately, the father's response was probably not the one he expected – 'Son you are always with me, and all that is mine is yours' (verse 31).

What the older son failed to recognise is that he has always had his inheritance. Everything that the father owns has been at his disposal, he has always been in the presence of the father and could always, at any time, have asked him for anything he needed or maybe even wanted. He has, in short, always been a son of the father, yet he has failed to recognise this. He has worked for an approval he already had and that the father may have never said he had to work for. He has been striving and toiling and trying to earn a love and acceptance that has always been there for him to enjoy and experience. He has been living to earn something which cannot be earned because it has already been given as a gift of grace. As a father, of course I want my children to do things to help out, but my love for them is not conditional on them doing those things. I know far too many people who have had to grow up trying to 'impress' their fathers, but I do not think that is a biblical view of fatherhood. Our kids should not have to earn our love or acceptance.

Striving verses Grace

Now, more than ever, this second son mentality has also become a picture of what people believe the church to be, certainly in the UK. In every church I have been part of, a large number of people are striving for God's approval. So many (too many) are putting service above the relationship with their Father. The danger is that serving in the church and ministry in general is so close to looking like a good thing, but is not the thing that we were primarily created for or that life as a Christian is about. We were made to be in relationship with the Father. Jesus did not die and rise again so that we can serve and serve to the full. Jesus makes it clear that He died and rose again so that we may have life and have it to the full (John 10:10). I am seeing far too many Christians putting their identity in what they *do* for God, rather than in the relationship they have *with* Him and who He is. It is not necessary, or even possible, to earn any more approval than we already have. It is called grace for a reason, and although that grace is outrageous and unbelievable at times, it is right at the heart of Paul's message to the Church in

Rome, especially in chapter 8. The message of grace is that we do not deserve it and it cannot be earned. The fact that we are saved, the very fact that you can call God 'Father', the whole Spirit of adoption that Paul speaks of, is an act of grace that we do not earn but we are called to accept. It is the thing that is so unbelievable that sometimes we fail to believe it, so end up working to achieve it. As Christopher Ash states, 'Whenever [God] rescued anyone, he did it 100 percent by grace, and they received it 100 percent by faith (and 0 percent by their own merit).'[9]

In his book *Jesus + Nothing = Everything*, Tullian Tchividjian describes how a revelation of our need for God's grace over our works, through a reading of Colossians, completely opened his eyes to the fact that we cannot earn God's approval. He calls our attempt to do so 'performancism', something that many Christians can fall foul of at times. Any acts of service we do should be in response to the fact that He has saved us and called us into relationship with the father, not in order that He will in the future. As Tullian states, 'The only thing you contribute to your salvation and to your sanctification is the sin that makes them necessary.'[10]

This sense of legalism, or that of earning the father's approval, is at the heart of why the older brother is envious of his younger sibling. He envies the freedom of relationship the other son now seems to possess, something that we perhaps glimpse in some of the religious leaders in Jesus' time, and no doubt Jesus intended for His hearers to pick up on this comparison. The people around Jesus were so focused on keeping to the rules that they often failed to see the miracles happening before their very eyes and, in many cases, also missed out on a relationship with the Son of God (see Mark 3:1-6).

We need to make sure that we do not become like this second son, that we don't become so focused on rules, regulations, obligations or religion that we miss the relationship that Jesus presents before us. Imagine if someone who wasn't a Christian walked into a church full of people like the second son! How put off would they be? Would you want to become part of a community that works so hard for their God's approval that they are exhausted or have no spare time for the people in their lives or for genuine and meaningful relationships? Would it inspire you to want a relationship with God if it looked like you had to earn it?

The reality is that you will never measure up, you will never 'do' enough, you will never serve enough to meet the ridiculously high standards that you may have set yourself somewhere along the line. If you try, like the older son, you will always be envious of the ones who find the freedom you have been striving for. This isn't what Jesus died for. Jesus died so that we can be free. Free to have a relationship with the father. God is far more interested in connection than correction.

Now picture the same person walking into a church where people are secure in their adopted identity. The people are still serving but not because they feel they must, but because they really want to. Obligation is not a word that features in such a church. There is a genuine love for community, for relationship. This is a group of people that because they are in a relationship with the Father, made possible by the Son and sealed by the Holy Spirit, have a model of relationship that they are able to show to others around them. They are not perfect, but that's OK! They know they will never measure up, which is why they are so thankful that Jesus has made them worthy, and is at work in them, making them more like Him. They still desire holiness, they still want to be the best versions of themselves that they can be, but at the same time they know they will make mistakes. Shame will not cause them to work any harder in order to try and earn forgiveness. These people know that God's mercies are new every morning (Lamentations 3:22-23). They know that the Spirit is working in them every day. This is an attractive community who have something that the visitor not only needs, but deeply desires, because it is what they have been looking for their entire lives. It may seem idealistic but this is, I believe, the kind of community we read about in Acts and that Paul is desiring the church in Rome to be like. It all stems from being absolutely secure in who we are and whose we are – we are God's chosen children.

Let us not be a church full people like the older son, let us be a church full of those who never take their new found, true freedom for granted, but who enjoy, embrace and live the life that is found in relationship with a father who loves them with a radical, outrageous and grace-fuelled love – the love of a perfect Father, who has adopted us into His family.

One of the primary roles of the Holy Spirit, at least according to Paul in his writing of Romans 8, is to help us to see that the prodigal son is more than just a story. It is a story that shows our status and identity as adopted sons and daughters of God, and it reveals the intimacy we can and do have with the father. The Spirit of adoption makes the prodigal son story our reality, and we learn that earning that adoption is something we cannot do on our own, but that we rely on the Father to do in us and for us.

Lord, thank you that you have chosen me. Thank you that you love me with an unconditional love. Thank you that you accept me as I am but love me too much to leave me that way. Thank you that you are at work in my life, making me more like Jesus. Help me not to strive for an approval I already have, but to give and serve from a place of thankfulness and to make my relationship with you, my perfect Father, my top priority in life. Help your church to know her identity in you, and may that security be a witness to those in search of theirs. Amen!

7 ABBA! FATHER!

by whom we cry 'Abba! Father!'

-8:15-

I have often been told the story of how I came to have the names that I have. Before I was born, my parents would regularly host international students in their home. My Mum often recounts how some of those students were more 'easy going' and nice to have around than some others, but it was always something they enjoyed doing. When my Mum was pregnant with me, they were hosting two German students, one called Karl and the other called Alexander. She remembers them as being the best students they ever had in their home. They were kind, helpful, polite and fun, and great with my two older brothers. So, when they bid farewell, they joked about naming me after them. That joke became a reality (although my Mum opted to take on the English spelling of my first name). My grandmother, however, has never been a fan of my first name, so for my entire life she has referred to me by my middle name. Even if I call her and say, "Hello, it's Carl," her response will always be, "Oh hello Alexander."

When parents name their children, some think carefully about meaning. We have four children, and each one is carefully named. Our name(s) can be very important to us, as well as important to those who gave them to us. In fact, there are a number of studies that suggest that a person's name is their favourite word or the sweetest sound to their ears. We like it when people remember our names, and it is something many people hope they can do and feel embarrassed about when they cannot. In the church I lead, we have one service a year where everyone wears a name label. There are so many people who have really appreciated this, often saying things like 'I'm so glad we did this today, I should know *N's* name by now, but it has been too embarrassing to ask.'

We also care a great deal about how people address us. As a father I would be disappointed if my children called me by name rather than 'Dad' or 'Daddy'. As an adopted child of God, I wonder how you address Him. When you pray, what names do you use for Him? There are no right or wrong answers to these questions, but how do you feel about calling Him your father? Does that term feel easy to you?

The term that Paul uses here is the same one that Jesus himself used when referring to God the Father, and encouraged us to use when teaching the Lord's Prayer. This word is a much more intimate term than 'father'. The word 'Abba' is one of the words that tends to get a little lost in translation, because it is an Aramaic word. Aramaic is such a poetic and symbolic language that our limited English language struggles to translate the meaning fully. The closest word we have in our language is the word 'Daddy'. 'Abba' is a word that traditionally would have been a term of endearment or intimacy, reserved only for people very close to you. The informality would have shocked the Jewish disciples as Jesus was teaching them the Lord's Prayer (Matthew 6:5-15) and would have come as a surprise to many of the new Christians in Rome who had converted from Judaism when Paul uses it here. It was not the 'done thing' to approach the great YHWH (Hebrew name for God) with such informality and intimacy. He was to be considered the one with an unpronounceable name, to be revered and feared as holy and righteous. God is still those things, but Paul is suggesting, as indeed Jesus did, that creating such intimacy between God and His children, is a key work of the Holy Spirit, and is the very thing Jesus came to make possible.

Father to Father

There are so many things about God that we simply do not understand. We have so many questions about why He does things the way He does, why He allows certain things to happen. There are profound mysteries about God that some have spent their entire lives trying to understand, to answer, or even begin to explain – but often they end up going around in circles having, at least in some cases, 'wasted' a lifetime of research trying to understand a God who really just wants us to know Him more than we understand Him.

I like the fact that there are things about God that are mysterious, things we do not understand and things that we may never know this side of heaven. To me, that makes Him more fascinating, more engaging, a more exciting father and more…well…God! There is, however, something that I have noticed recently. When it comes to using analogies to explain God to other people, I am (more often than not) finding myself using the analogy of parenthood, and in particular, my own experiences of being a father.

It makes sense when I think about it – as God is the perfect father, it is logical that when one becomes a parent, one can see the parallels and begin to understand God as father a little more. I was talking to a father recently who said, "becoming a father has helped me to realise how much my parents did for me and the sacrifices they made." How much more so is this likely to be the case with our understanding of God. I can never profess to have all the answers to all the mysteries but there are some things that being a father has helped me to make a little more sense of.

As I learn to love my children more, it makes sense that love, at times, can be a choice.

As I seek to discipline my children in the best way, it makes sense of why God would want to discipline us.

As I try to help our children to have healthy boundaries in order to keep them safe and to see them thrive, it makes sense why God would give His children the commandments.

As we have people round for dinner and we desire for our children to be polite and to represent the family well, it makes sense why God wants His children to be set apart.

As I love my children and long for their love in return, it makes sense why God would make loving Him the highest call.

As I, at times, let my children make mistakes to learn right from wrong (hard as it is to watch sometimes), it makes sense why God would give us free will.

As there are times when I can't step in as a parent to help a child suffering and all I can do is hold them, it makes sense of how God feels to see us suffer.

As I love to treat my children, it makes sense why God is so gracious and generous.

As I smile inside and out when I hear my children laugh, it makes sense that the joy of the Lord is our strength.

As I see our children having fun with great friends, it makes sense why Jesus would gift us with the church and community.

As I say 'no' to my children when they ask for something they don't necessarily need or that could harm them, it makes sense why God doesn't always answer prayers the way we might want Him to.

As I rejoice when a child chooses to put down what they are doing in order to come and do something with me, it makes sense why God is delighted when we give Him time and make Him our priority.

As I try to create a home in which my children are happy, settled and safe, it makes sense why God wants to renew the whole of creation.

As I love to see our children grow and mature, it makes sense why discipleship is so important and why God never wants us to become 'stuck' in our faith.

As I ask my children to trust me even if they don't know what is happening, it makes sense that faith and trust go hand in hand and that you can't have one without the other.

As I look forward to quality time with my children on a day off, it makes sense that God would give us the Sabbath to spend with Him – and that He would make it law.

As I referee fights between siblings and enjoy the moments when they play well together or support each other, it makes sense of God's desire for unity.

As I learn to communicate with our children in ways that they appreciate individually, it makes sense that God would speak in so many different ways.

As I have moments when I am fun, serious, fast, slow, teaching them, showing them, guiding them, whispering, talking and even shouting, it makes sense that God would reveal Himself in so many different ways.

As I seek to find new ways to surprise my children and do things they have never seen me do before, it makes sense that the Holy Spirit would do amazing and sometimes puzzling things in worship and in our lives generally.

As I think about the fact that I would do anything to keep my children safe, to keep them close and to keep our relationship possible and open, it makes sense of the cross.

As I seek to forgive my children and bless them, even if they 'don't deserve it', it makes sense of grace.

As I withhold certain things about myself from my children until they are old enough to understand, it makes sense of the mystery of God.

It is important that you know that I am not saying that you have to become a father in order to understand these things. For me, being a father has helped me to grasp these mysteries of God the Father a little more, and to understand them in new ways, which in turn has helped me to teach others about Him. Ultimately, as I try to be the best father that I can be (and even through my mistakes as a father) it makes sense why I need Him as my perfect father, why knowing Him intimately as Abba Father, Daddy God, helps me, and why my life without Him would be meaningless.

Who is my Father?

Over the years that I have been a Christian I have come across a number of brothers and sisters in Christ who struggle with the concept of God being their father. They can happily accept that Christ died for them, that He is their saviour, king, and brother. Some accept the Holy Spirit in their lives, and love Him and what

He does. In spite of this, they still struggle to call God their father in any formal way, let alone in the intimate way that Jesus invites us to.

When people struggle with this concept they may ignore, and in some cases completely reject, the idea of God being the father that He is. This can lead to some forms of theology that seek to entirely replace the notion of God as father – either with the idea that God has no gender at all, or even to suggest that God is more of a mother than a father. Being completely honest, this is something that I have struggled with for some time. I know that may be an unpopular thought for some readers, but it is an honest reflection.

I do understand that there are people who have had such terrible experiences of earthly fathers that the concept of God being a father is a very hard one to live with, and so to ease their relationship with God, some may find it easier to view God as non-gendered or female. Equally I have known people who have had difficult or non-existent relationships with their mothers and have found this theology equally difficult to swallow. I do know of people who have come to faith only when they have been able to picture God as something other than a father. Whilst this is all understandable from a pastoral point of view, it still seems (to me at least) that there is something very fundamental about God as father that gets lost when any substitution takes place.

The issue we face is that we tend to only be able to relate to God as father by using our earthly experiences of fatherhood as a guide. Many seem to only be able to project their human experience of father, good or bad, onto God when relating to Him in this capacity. Images and memories associated with the word 'father' fill our minds of life experiences when we hear it, and can cause an invisible wall between us and God. Whilst it is true that the term will instantly cause us to remember those experiences and we will naturally project them onto God, I also believe it can be possible to move in some way beyond those projections and have a clearer view of God as father.

It is important to note that the projections don't only happen when we have negative experiences of fatherhood, the same can also be true for those with positive experiences of fathers, even if a loved father is no longer alive. I have known Christians who have felt guilty for even considering God as a father, and will do all they can to ensure that God doesn't 'replace' the earthly father they loved so much. This can seem a bit like God being the 'step-father' or 'second father' who has come in to the family setting. I have not only known other Christians for whom this is the case, this has also been true for me.

I have been blessed enough to have a very positive relationship with my Dad. We have always got on well. He worked shifts a lot when I was younger, but he more than made up for that time when he was around and he invested well into me and my two older brothers. He was and is ever present, generous, and kind, and is now proving to be an amazing Grandad to all our children. But even such a positive experience caused tensions for me when I first came to faith as a teenager. One of the great things about my dad was that he would always let us choose the music in the car. For the most part, when it was my choice, it would be a Queen album so we were both equally happy with that. When I came to faith, however, I began listening to worship music. I remember on one particular journey a song about God being the perfect father came on. I was singing at first but then stopped and I distinctly remember thinking that I didn't want my Dad to feel 'replaced' by God.

So yes, we can and do project. Yes, our earthly experiences, positive or negative, can have an effect on how we relate to God, but I also believe that there is a clear picture of God as the *perfect* father in scripture, and also in the life stories of people for whom healing in the areas where earthly fathers have let them down has been found in God as perfect father. It is possible to move beyond those projections. One of the questions that we can ask ourselves to help with this is: 'Who was my father first?'

I believe that my earthly father only had me because a creator God, whose very nature is that of a father, had conceived the idea first. He is the father who knit me together in my mother's womb (see Psalm 139). He is the one who has been with me since before my birth, calling me into relationship with Him. He has been the only true constant in my life. This is true for all of us, even at the times when our earthly fathers may have failed us or let us down, by choice or by circumstance. He is the father who absolutely chose you by adoption and sent His son to make this possible. He is the father who stands outside of time, so although you may only know Him as father when you accept His gift of grace, He has been your father since the beginning of time. It is a mystery, it is mind blowing, and hard to grasp, especially in light of the adoption that Paul speaks of in Romans, but God was, is, and has always been your father first. He has entrusted you to an earthly father.

We do find God referred to as 'father' in the Old Testament, albeit less often than in the New Testament. He is quoted by the psalmist as being a father of nations, and he is referred to as a father in other texts by the prophets. But God desires to not just be a father in theological terms, or by reference, but He has a deep desire to be a father that we can relate to, be in relationship with and learn from – a father that you can have closeness with. He is the father who knows you better than anyone else, better, even, than you know yourself, because you are made in His image, with His fingerprints. He has loved you since before the beginning of time, in ways that no earthly father would know how to. God was, is, and has always been your father first.

Nothing in this world breaks my heart more than hearing of earthly fathers who have abused the privilege that God has given them to care for His children. It baffles me that a father could ever do anything to harm one of his own children (or any child for that matter). Some father wounds, however, are not caused deliberately. The reality is that all fathers fail on some level. This isn't to make dads feel guilty, it is just a reality that we can never be everything that our children need us to be. We can seek to be the best version of ourselves that we can be. We can remember and try to live by important truths like 'the best gift a father can give to his children is to love their mum' or 'being present is the best present you can give', but there will be times when fathers let their children down, where they can't be there for that significant moment, or simply will make mistakes.

There is no such thing as a perfect father. This does not excuse those who cause major harm, but it reminds us that there is a need in this world (and I think now more than ever before) for a relationship with a perfect heavenly father who can heal those wounds, who can be and is perfect, who will never let us down. What the world needs is not to replace God the father with a more acceptable persona, what the world needs is to discover the healing for their wounds in the perfect, unfailing, creator God in whose image they were made, before anyone else had the idea to have them. You need to know that He was your father long before anyone on earth was – and more than that, He is the father who chose you and delights in you and longs for you to be free of any pain caused by those who raised you, so that you can become the best version of yourself that you can be, raised by a perfect heavenly father. And those of us who are fathers, can also learn a thing or two from Him as we seek to care for the children that He has entrusted to our care.

In no way am I seeking to undermine the pain caused by some fathers on earth in this broken world in which we live. I fully acknowledge that for some, moving on from father wounds can take many years. Counselling may be needed, but replacing God with another persona will only ever be a bandage to cover a symptom. True, deep healing can only be found in the knowledge that this father is the one who the Bible says He is and you are who He says you are – a beloved, chosen, adopted son or daughter of a perfect Daddy God. If you struggle with that level of intimacy, then rather than replacing, why not ask 'What do I need to deal with in my life to help me see God as my father?' If you believe that Jesus is who He says He is, and you believe Him to be a truthful person, then look at how He describes the Father in John 15 – see how much He desires for you to know the Father.

It is also important to note, as Paul does, the role of the Holy Spirit in all of this. It is only possible to cry 'Abba! Father!' with the Spirit's help. He is beautifully intertwined with God the Father and Jesus the Son, and He longs to draw us into that relationship and to understand our place within it. I have heard countless people, who for many years had a particular view of God, say that when they had a life-transforming encounter with the Holy Spirit, the father heart of God was revealed to them, often for the first time. These encounters have changed their lives and deepened their relationships with God. How we view God has the power to change everything for us. Don't replace the Father with some other persona – do all you can to know Him as the father that He longs to be for you, and if you ask the Spirit to help, He is ready and waiting to do so.

Abba! Father, Daddy God, thank you that you have always been my father first. Thank you that you are the one true constant in my life. Thank you that you chose me. Help me to see you as the father that you are.

Help me to find the healing I need so that I can fully embrace you as my perfect heavenly father.

May I come to know you the way that Jesus knows you. Bless and help all the fathers of this world — may they reflect your love in how they raise your precious children.

Holy Spirit, show me the heart of the Father. Amen!

8 NO LONGER SLAVES

For you did not receive the spirit of slavery to fall back into fear.

-8:15-

I am someone who has a very addictive nature. I find myself feeling very grateful for the things that I have not become addicted to over the years – there are things that I have deliberately avoided trying in case they lead to addiction, and there are things that could be addictive that I simply (by the grace of God) do not have a taste for. For me though, there are still addictions and they can still be damaging. I can easily become addicted to collecting things. As a child it was sticker albums (I say 'as a child' but I have also collected these as an adult). You may think that this isn't a bad addiction but I discovered recently that the average collector spends between £350 and £500 per collection of cards or stickers. When I have collected in the past, I have definitely become a slave to that addiction. I would arrange shopping trips around the places that I knew sold what I was collecting. I wouldn't be able to step into a shop without buying something to add to that collection and I wouldn't be satisfied until the collection was complete. Then comes the day that the final card is collected and there comes the feeling of disappointment and emptiness and shame at the money I have spent (wasted) on something that now just sits in a folder somewhere on one of my bookshelves, and of the ones I collected as a kid, possibly somewhere in my parent's loft, gathering dust.

If it is not collecting something, then completing things is something that I become a slave to. I have been known to waste hours on games that are probably never meant to be completed. At times I would neglect time with my kids, or my wife, or even time with God, as I got drawn in to the kind of games where you set something up and from that point you are enslaved, checking back every hour or so, to make sure you complete the tasks that are set as efficiently as possible.

I know these may seem like trivial examples, but they are things that have enslaved me, trapped me and stunted the part of me that was made to thrive with God and with others, as they have robbed me of time, finances and focus. You may not relate to these particular examples, but we all have at some time in our lives been slaves to something. Paul speaks about us being 'slaves to sin' (Romans 6:20), there are, however, many other things that fall within the definition of slavery. If you are addicted to anything then you are enslaved. If you are forced to submit to someone, then you are enslaved. If you are living in debt and are having to spend every penny you earn paying off those debts, then you are enslaved.

When we are enslaved by these things, we find that fear is closely linked to that slavery; that is why Paul says that the spirit of fear is to do with slavery. Fear and slavery are very intertwined and they are both symptoms of sin and being in a broken, fallen world and separated from our Father. This is why the Spirit of adoption is crucial in our salvation and is the perfect antidote to slavery, and the fear that goes with it.

The Perfect Antidote

The Spirit of adoption is more than just about our status and identity as it provides this perfect antidote to fear. The question is: how? When Paul was writing, slavery was very much commonplace in the Roman world. It was a social and ethical norm. Some of Jesus' teaching and Paul's writing dealt with the corruption surrounding it, and encouraged Christian slave owners to be ethical, moral and, therefore, set apart from the rest of the known world in how they treated their slaves, but slavery was still very much the norm. Over time, slavery has become more and more corrupt and less and less acceptable and thanks to the work of one of my heroes of the faith, William Wilberforce, it is no longer legal in the UK. Sadly, however, it does still happen, and there are places around the world where it is still acceptable. But I am fairly confident that much of the readership of this book will be made up of people who have little to no first-hand experience of slavery.

As has already been highlighted, slavery is an illustration we can still relate to as we have all been slaves to something, if nothing else, we have been slaves to sin. The thing I have found is that when I am enslaved I need someone to rescue me, to show me that it is not the norm. I need someone to lift my gaze, to re-align my priorities. Sometimes I may need a gentle nudge or reminder. At other times I will need a strong wake-up call, a challenge, and sometimes maybe even a kick up the backside. I need someone to help me to stop bowing down to the master of my slavery. Once what is enslaving us has been noticed and named, we can begin to address the issue. The reality is, however, that the hold that these things have over us can go largely unnoticed in our lives. Even when we do notice them, there are many things that can be so hard to walk free from, or to no longer allow to hold us captive as slaves. But why do we find it so hard to do this?

Again, I think this has something to do with the fear that can be attached to the slavery. We can be fearful of losing out, fearful of not knowing what we would be without this thing that is giving us 'purpose'. Perhaps we can be fearful of judgement if we expose our need for help to others. Perhaps we are fearful that we can never be free, or that the slave master will always find us and pull us back. All of these fears are closely and strongly linked to our identity. This ultimately makes us a slave to fear, way above being a slave to any addiction. It can almost be as though fear is the real slave master and the things that we are addicted to, are his employees whose job it is to keep us distracted from reality, and God, for long enough to not see the grip that fear has. But fear is not only linked to addictions. There are so many things in life that can cause fear to dominate our lives. Whatever the root or the cause of our fear, it takes over when we forget who we really are. This is why we need the antidote of adoption – it is in this place that we are reminded we no longer need to be slaves to fear.

No Longer a Slave to Fear

Some fear is good. Some fear is there to protect us from danger and from harm. It is quite sensible to be afraid of heights in some way because that fear stops most of us from jumping off high places (without something to slow down or stop our fall). Fear will keep us at arm's length from a fierce predator and protect us from all kinds of dangers. The slavery to fear occurs when we allow such a fear to dominate our landscape. I may be naturally afraid of heights for protection but when that fear moves from being something that keeps me away from the edge, to something that stops me going anywhere near any kind of high place then the fear is dominating my life. When it stops me from doing something I might otherwise enjoy, it has become my master. My life decisions are made by that fear. It can cripple us when this happens, stop us in our tracks and rob us of joy and peace.

At times fear can even cause us to lose sight of the certainty of the gospel truth. I always thought I had experienced this kind of fear in my life. Recently, however, I really did! There have been times in my life I have been nervous, or maybe even a little scared by things, and there have been times when those nerves may have held me back from doing something that I later discovered were fun. There are situations that make me worried, but it was only very recently that I was 'gripped by fear' – an expression I was aware of but, in hindsight, don't remember feeling before.

It was a Thursday night in the school holidays. I had been suffering for a couple of weeks with a sore shoulder, I had a doctor's appointment due but there was a bit of a wait so I was just finding ways to cope with the pain. On one particular night the pain got worse, then it spread across to my chest, I felt a little breathless and I don't know if I was imagining it, but my left arm went a bit numb. My mind instantly went to a dark place. A place where I was wondering if this was the start of some kind of heart failure. Suddenly I was experiencing a fear I had never experienced before. I was too anxious to sleep in the fear that something might happen, but at the same time I was so scared of what it could be and the consequences on my family of me having to be rushed to hospital in the night that I did nothing about it – nothing except for worry, imagine, plan, process – often fear does seem to disable our logical thinking!! I tried praying but felt no less fearful. Eventually I fell asleep on the sofa at around 2:30am. I woke up a few hours later (feeling glad that I had) and phoned a UK helpline for medical advice. They gave me some reassurance that it didn't sound like a heart problem but advised me to see a GP within the next few hours. Still holding on to some of this fear, I rang the surgery and got an appointment for later that day. But fear clung to me like a disease, and I became a slave to it and those fears were not relieved until the moment I got an 'OK' from the doctor.

In that night, I was certainly a slave to fear, completely gripped by it. There were, however, moments of peace within that fear. One of the clearest memories I have of that night was of thinking, 'if this is it, if this is my time, then God, I trust you to care for my family.' For that brief moment I explored an area of trust I had never really had to consider before – trusting God with my family, my health and even my own life. In that moment I had a security. And that security didn't come from my circumstances or anything that God said to me. It came from a realisation of an perspective-changing truth – in that moment I had a security in the knowledge that as good as a father I may try to be, He can be and is the perfect father for all of my family, the same perfect father I have known Him to be for me. He was, after all, their father first, and whilst I really want to be their father and to see them grow old, if that was to no longer be the case then they would still have the best father that any child (or adult) could ever hope for. They would have questions for Him, they may even be angry at Him, but I knew, absolutely knew, in that moment, that He would care for them as He does for me. I can't say that this thought or reminder of truth was enough to take all my fear away, but it led me to want to listen to a talk online as I continued to wrestle with my fear, or rather to distract me from it.

Whilst listening to that talk in the middle of the night, a talk about closeness with the father, I was able to allow sleep to take over – I was secure in the knowledge that God, my perfect Father, knew what He was doing. He knew if I would wake up or not and, as my father, He would be beside me, as well as being beside and with the ones I love – every step, in every moment. This came from the knowledge of what Paul writes here. That I am adopted by a perfect father. The reminder of the truth of who I am and whose I am, loosened the grip that fear had.

When I look back on that experience now, I can't really tell if that fear was rational or not. I know that it gripped me and made me its slave for the night. What helped me was not an increased awareness of what God was doing, but rather of who my father is, and just how much He loves me. In 1 John 4:18 we read that 'there is no fear in love' and that perfect love has the power to drive out all fear. It is a popular verse for weddings, but in reality, the love that we have for one another may have the power to only reduce fear – there is only one perfect love that has the power to drive it out. The Holy Spirit, the Spirit of adoption, is the only one with that power. Only He can so remind us of God's love for us, that we are overwhelmed by that love in such a way that fear simply doesn't have room at the inn. When you are loved, and know that you are loved, you feel safer. You know that your champion will do everything they can do to protect you. When we know we are loved it gives us a sense of security, acceptance, peace, connection, of being chosen and that we are important to someone else. How much more is this the case when we know the perfect love of the perfect Father who has chosen and adopted us?

Fear is often fuelled by uncertainty. We can often fear what we do not know and can feel more fearful when outcomes or futures are unknown. This uncertainty can play right into the hands of our fear. This is the area that God's perfect love can speak into – because His love comes with absolute certainty; certainty of who we are, certainty of whose we are, even certainty of what awaits us beyond this life. We need not even fear death. Having such a certain hope and certain identity in a perfect Father causes fear to lose its power over us. The more aware we become of God's love for us, the more we allow His love into our lives, the less room there is for fear – and so, sometimes over time, sometimes instantly, that fear is cast out altogether by the strength and power of His perfect love. His love, by His Spirit, has the ability to overwhelm what overwhelms you. His perfect love can cast out all fear – and we can be secure in this love because it comes from a father who has chosen to make us His own. We are sons and daughters and no longer slaves. We no longer need to serve that master of fear because we have a Father of love instead!

We may still experience fear, some things are scary, and some fear is there to protect us. The difference that Jesus makes though, is that fear no longer has the power to control us. It no longer has the power to dominate the landscape of our lives. It doesn't have the power to maintain a grip once we let God remind us of His love, power and victory over the source of that fear.

God can also use fear to throw us into His arms. It can help us to acknowledge our need of Him and dependence upon Him. It can become an opportunity for us to learn more about His gentleness as well as His power, His kindness and His faithfulness. What this means is that not only are we no longer slaves to fear but fear has become a slave of our Father. So next time you find yourself feeling fearful try to remind yourselves of these truths and allow His perfect love to cast out that fear.

I should also add that my heart is fine and I am still alive, all by the grace of God, and whilst I hope I never experience fear like that again, I am glad of the lessons that night taught me and the place of surrender and trust it led me too – fear can serve my God!

God, I thank you that I no longer need to be a slave to fear, because I am a child of God. Help me in those areas of my life where I may have given in to fear. Speak truth and life into those situations and circumstances that overwhelm me, and may you overwhelm them to such an extent that your perfect love is able to cast out all fear. Amen!

9 IF OUR GOD IS FOR US...

What then shall we say to these things? If God is for us, who can be against us?

-8:31-

Have you ever experienced what it feels like to be supported, to be cheered on and to have a champion? Growing up, our family was a tenpin bowling family. Both of my parents had always been into the sport to the point that the local bowling alley became known as our second home. There were people there who watched me grow up, who smiled and 'aahhhed' when I threw my first bowling ball (between my legs as a four-year-old). My brothers and I were all part of the children's and then youth bowling clubs. At the age of 10, I had my first coach – he was great! Always willing me to do well, and he made coaching sessions enjoyable so I always learnt a lot from him.

I remember one particular Saturday, I must have been about 12 at the time. I had been selected to represent our centre's youth bowling club, along with about seven others, at a national event. It was my first tournament away from home. Parents were not permitted to come on the trip with us so, waving goodbye, the minibus set off for a long journey. We had great fun on the way, fellow team mates, coaches and others who had come to help and support us. I was so excited when we arrived. I was chosen to play in the team event and the doubles event. My team event did not go so well for me. Later in the afternoon we had the doubles event and I was paired with a very good friend of mine. We always enjoyed bowling together and would often bring the best out of each other. My first two games were OK and I was bowling around my usual average, and certainly better than I had earlier in the day. Then came the last game. The match was close and my team mate had just bowled an game. I was bowling pretty well too, despite the machines breaking down a couple of times. Due to the delays, all the other matches that were playing around us had finished, whilst we were about half way through our final game. As a result, all of my fellow team mates, as well as many others, had gathered around our lanes to see how this final game would end and affect the final results.

A few frames in I knew things were going well for me. I was getting lots of spares (feel free to look up the rules of the game if you have no idea what I am talking about) and a few strikes too. It was the final frame, I needed seven for our team to win and anything above that would have scored me my first ever 200 game. I could feel, sense even, the support of my friends and team mates behind me. I bowled the ball, it seemed to take forever to make it to the pins. I got nine – so we won the game and I got 202, my first ever 200 game (just). I was ecstatic, and I turned around to see everyone else was too. It was amazing to see other people happy *for me* as well as with me. The joy continued as word of my achievement reached back home and all those who had come to welcome the team home cheered as I got off the bus, trophies in hand, smile wider than ever.

Their accolades felt good. I felt supported, encouraged, valued, but that was only because I had done something good. If I had knocked over six pins with that last ball, I would to some degree have still had their support 'well done Carl, you tried your best' or 'better luck next time.' As it was, the praise lasted a couple of weeks but then faded when the next person had their great achievement. (Indecently I bowled another 200 game two weeks later, but it was during training so no one was there to see it.)

The concept of God being *for us* though, far outruns this kind of transitory support that depends on you doing well. God is always your champion. He is willing you on to do well, to be well, to be the best version of yourself that you can possibly be. He is always coaching, guiding, showing, teaching, encouraging, revealing truth and cheering you on. And even if you only knock over six, or even if you miss the mark completely, He is still for you. Even if you fall off the wagon, slip back into those old ways, give in to temptation, or miss your daily time with Him, He is still for you, and He always will be. His championing does not rely on your performance – He's for you, because He is for you!

It's funny, but in that moment on those bowling lanes, when I was so aware of the support I had, I was no longer influenced in my bowling by the opposing team. I wasn't threatened by the scores I had to achieve for the win or for that high score. I was aware of the target and very aware that they were a better team than us on paper, but I wasn't focused on what I needed to achieve. I was in the moment, in the now, carried by the love and support of others, willing me to do well. The same can be true when we focus on our champion rather than on what seeks to overwhelm us.

Knowing me, Knowing you

When you know whose you are, and you know that your perfect heavenly Father is for you and being your champion, then who or what can stand against such knowledge of such life-transforming truth? You have God, the same God that made the universe, on your side, in your corner, on your team. This verse does not mean that you will never have enemies or opposition (in fact other passages would suggest that the opposite is true) but it does mean that *nothing* can ever rob you of the fact that you are a child of God. No circumstance, no suffering, no pain, no struggle can stop you from being His chosen, adopted child. If you have a life-altering diagnosis, you are still an heir of the Kingdom. If you can't do the things you would like to be able to do due to ill health or old age, you are still a loved and valued son or daughter of God. If you struggle with addiction, you are still loved unconditionally. If you have doubts, you are still adored. If you make mistakes, have regrets, if you've been wronged, if you are broken or hurting, you are still a precious, loved, adored, chosen, died for, child of a perfect heavenly Father – a father who is for you – and nothing can come against that truth. There is nowhere better from which to view the circumstances of life, than from the lap of a father God who is, and will always be, your champion.

For me, one of the best examples we have of the fact that God is for us and not against us is the gift of the Church. He knows that we were made to be in community, as He himself is perfect community. He knows we need each other, and one of the greatest needs we have is the need to be able to remind each other about God's faithfulness – this is why gathered worship is so important. This is why, for so many people in this world, having that taken away by a global pandemic in 2020-1 had a huge impact on their mental and spiritual health. We know that God can be found in all things and can be worshiped anywhere. We know we don't need church to be close to God, or to serve God. The pandemic has seen the church rise up in amazing ways to 'be' the church and to serve those in need. The reality is, however, that we still need community. In Paul's letter to the Ephesians he urges us to pray for all the saints. It is in this context of prayer that he introduces the armour of God as a concept for us to grasp hold of in our life of faith and prayer – it's here we see that God is not only our champion, cheering us on, but is actually fighting on our behalf.

Finally, be strong in the Lord and in the strength of his might. Put on the whole armour of God, that you may be able to stand against the schemes of the devil. For we do not wrestle against flesh and blood, but against the rulers, against the authorities, against the cosmic powers over this present darkness, against the spiritual forces of evil in the heavenly places. Therefore, take up the whole armour of God, that you may be able to withstand in the evil day, and having done all, to stand firm. Stand therefore, having fastened on the belt of truth, and having put on the breastplate of righteousness, and, as shoes for your feet, having put on the readiness given by the gospel of peace. In all circumstances take up the shield of faith, with which you can extinguish all the flaming darts of the evil one; and take the helmet of salvation, and the sword of the Spirit, which is the word of God, praying at all times in the Spirit, with all prayer and supplication. To that end, keep alert with all perseverance, making supplication for all the saints, and also for me, that words may be given to me in opening my mouth boldly to proclaim the mystery of the gospel, for which I am an ambassador in chains, that I may declare it boldly, as I ought to speak. (Ephesians 6:10-20).

I am not going to go into a full exegesis about each element of the armour of God and what they mean – but this passage makes it clear that in the spiritual battles that we face, our perfect heavenly Father, who is for us and not against us, has equipped us with everything we need to stand, whilst He has fought and is fighting the battle for us. Our call is only to stand firm – He does the rest. That said, we are still affected by the battles that rage around us and sometimes against us. There is one thing to note about the armour – the only part of us that is exposed is the back. This is where God knows that we need each other – to ensure that our backs are covered by one another. This means that if we are tempted to turn away from God, or if in weakness we let our guard down in some way, there are others to help us stand firm.

It makes sense that when someone is wronged by a church community it can cause so much pain and grief. Our churches should be life-giving, faith-enhancing places where we can gather with those who will champion us in our faith. There are some who would try to say that they don't need to go to church to be a Christian, but I believe that whilst it is possible to have faith in Jesus without going to church, I don't believe it is possible to sustain that faith without our brothers and sisters in Christ around us, reminding us, when we face trials, to stand firm in the knowledge that God is for us and not against us. Our brothers and sisters in Christ can help us to stand when we don't have the strength to. They can challenge us when we let our guard down, or let temptations get the better of us, to remind us that nothing can separate us from God's love. Is the church perfect? No. If you think you have found the perfect church, then, as the saying goes, you have already ruined it by walking in. Churches are made up of people – messy, broken, fallen people – so of course they are not perfect and the church will get things wrong. We need to be aware that no community will ever be perfect, but we should be asking 'how is this community reminding me that God is for me?' Or what may be even more important to ask is 'what am I doing to help people in this community to know, beyond any shadow of doubt, that God is for them, with them, championing them and fighting for them?' Through the pandemic and lockdowns in the UK and other nations we had to be truly imaginative about how to do this, but many were able to prove that it was still possible even when we couldn't meet physically.

A truly united church, a church that is united despite differences, is a powerful weapon in God's arsenal. A church that is Holy Spirit filled and fuelled is one that knows our need for Jesus, and our need for one another to help us in our relationship with Him. This kind of fellowship reminds us that when we face trials we are on the winning side, because our perfect heavenly Father – the one who made everything, the one who is sovereign over all – is our champion! And if He is for us, then who or what could possibly be against us? Some people may give you the illusion that they can stand against you, the enemy might try to convince you of the lie that he can, but the truth is NO-ONE and NOTHING ever can come between you and God's love for you!

It is a great thing, and a gift, to have a community to remind us of these truths, but we also have countless testimonies in scripture of God's power, strength and ability to save. We also have stories of where God has done the seemingly impossible for His people. We have the victory of the cross, and the death-defeating resurrection. We have the, often overlooked, ascension that reminds us of God's rule and reign over all and the authority given to Jesus who is seated at God's right hand. We have the truth of the epistles as early church fathers encouraged people in their faith, and we have chapters like Romans 8 to remind us of our status as God's own children, whom He has moved heaven and earth to be in relationship with. We have all the promises of all that He will do when He comes again, and the promise of eternity. We are in relationship with an incredibly powerful God. That's our Dad! He is on our side, He is our champion and we are on His winning team.

There are spiritual forces who are deluded or desperate enough to try and stand against us and even try and stand against Him. There are others who think that if they can't get to Him they will try to get to Him through us, seeking to deplete His army. They don't need to destroy us, just distract us enough, to sow enough doubt in our identity to weaken us. They do this because they know that when we truly know and believe that we are children of God and are secure in our identity, when we know and truly believe whose side we are on and who our champion is, we are powerful – because we know that nothing, in heaven or on earth, can stand against those who are children of God. Children who are filled with the same power that rose Jesus from the grave. Those people are more than conquerors. I make no apology for labouring a point in this chapter – if you still don't believe this truth, then read it again and ask yourself this one question: 'How secure am I in the knowledge that nothing can separate me from the love of God?'

Victory vs Disappointment

None of this means that we are free from struggle or even disappointment. It does not allow us to form any false sense of victory. We still live in a fallen, broken world. There will be people who oppose us or the Jesus we love and serve. There will be people who come against us and against the church we are part of. They will come against the community that God intended for good and His bride, the church, will receive a bad press. Divisions will happen because of our fallenness, and those looking on will criticise our faith. Persecution will continue to be a reality for the church in some places. These things may well come against us in a very human sense. Wars, pandemics and divisions will still happen. They will be very real problems and may have physical consequences on our worship and maybe even our safety. But they cannot come against our identity as children of God. This is why true victory, for the Christian, is the ability to stand strong in the face of such opposition. Our victory is not found in defeating the enemy but in knowing that Jesus already has. Our power is found not in a change of circumstances but a change in our attitude towards them. It is the ability, in the face of any opposition, to be able to say 'It is well with my soul.' It is the ability to declare the words of Psalm 46:1-3, from any place: 'God is our refuge and strength, a very present help in trouble. Therefore, will not we fear, though the earth gives way, though the mountains be moved into the heart of the sea; though its waters roar and foam, though the mountains tremble at its swelling.' We can be secure and steadfast in the knowledge that the victory has already been won for us by Christ on the cross, and in that He has secured our identity as sons and daughters of God, heirs of the Kingdom, and even death itself cannot change this. That is where our true victory is found.

There will be times it seems that God doesn't answer our prayers. There will be seasons that we don't receive the 'victory' we were hoping for. These times can lead to a tremendous sense of disappointment. It can be easy to focus on what God hasn't done or isn't doing. If we are honest with ourselves and with God, we have probably all experienced this at some point in our faith journey (although we may not like to admit it). We need to ensure we do all we can in order not to stay in that place of disappointment (it can be the breeding ground of cynicism and frustration). We need to move to a place of trust and thankfulness. Even if we feel we are unable to do so, it is possible, from that place of disappointment (using the help of others if needed) to remind ourselves where our true victory is found – in Christ. Not in what is happening, not in a change to our circumstances, not in the removal of the cause of our disappointment, but in who God is and what He *has* done and what *we know* He can do. Like many things to do with our faith, our victory is found not in something physical but in the person of Jesus Christ and our relationship with Him!

Father God, I thank you for being my champion, for not only supporting me, but also fighting for me. Thank you for the people you have put in my life to help me to know and remember the truth of who you are and whose I am. Help me to truly know that there is nothing that can stand against me, because my Father God is for me

Thank you for being my champion. Amen!

10 ALL THINGS

And we know that for those who love God all things work together for good, for those who are called according to his purpose.

-8:28-

Hindsight can be a wonderful thing. It can also be a burden. If you are anything like me, you can come up with the perfect response just as you are walking away from the conversation, and you kick yourself for not thinking of it at the time.

It is amazing how different things can seem from alternative perspectives. I don't know if you have ever been up the Eiffel Tower in Paris, but even if you haven't, it is obvious to say that the view from the bottom is very different from the one at the top. In order to appreciate the view from the top, the stairs need to be climbed. As you climb the steps you will get glimpses of the view to come but you will not see it in its entirety until the final destination has been reached. It is from the top that you can look and see not only a new perspective, but you are also able to look down to see how far you have come, what climbing those stairs has achieved (unless you got the lift, but the principle is the same).

There are times that our lives can feel a bit like that climb. We can go through an experience we don't understand, perhaps something that is hard work, perhaps a time where all we can see is the next step in front of us, maybe even times where we can't even see that. It can feel like we are stuck. We want a short cut out of the situation but the lift is out of order and the only choice that seems available to us is to climb. Other people seem to be climbing with no problem, leaping up the stairs one or two steps at a time, or we may compare ourselves to those already at the top and feel like it will never be like that for us. We believe we will never feel the freedom that they feel. We may feel like we should go backwards and back to what we know, the solid ground beneath. We may become frustrated at those moving faster than us and not stopping to help, and we may even blame God for the fact that we are having to climb and that we can't just be at the top. It is always possible to take an analogy too far, but I am sure there may be some recognition here in how you have felt at times in your faith journey or life as a whole.

The reality is that suffering and struggle are part of life, but this particular verse is not referring just to suffering. Paul is stating that *all* things work together, that means the bad things yes, but also the good things, the experiences, the challenges, the changes, the moments of grief and sorrow, and the moments of joy and laughter, the times of financial security and crippling debt. This verse is not about God turning situations around to make them good, but about Him using circumstances, experiences and life generally, for good. It is about Him drawing good from every situation rather than about Him making all things good.

Before I came to faith, I had a good and comfortable life. I was enjoying what I was doing in school, I had a direction in life, and was training to be a sports coach, and was happy with that plan. I was enjoying my training and the courses I was going on and was looking forward to the challenge. I was particularly enjoying coaching young people, and was doing a lot of work with schools to help with their sports. This plan changed when I had my calling to ordained ministry, but the training wasn't wasted – little did I know that I would later become a schools worker for Jesus. He worked that previous experience for good.

When I started secondary school, I was quite a shy and reserved child. I loved to sing (privately) and enjoyed music. A teacher once overheard me singing and encouraged me to audition for the school musical he was producing. The next week I auditioned for a part in the chorus but was offered the role of the wizard in *The Wizard of Oz*. This led to me performing in a different musical every year for the rest of my time at secondary school. I became much more confident in front of groups of people, and developed my voice. There was nothing spiritual about these musicals, but neither I, nor that teacher, could have foreseen that I would later become a worship leader and preacher for Jesus, using the confidence and skills I developed for good and for God.

All things really do work together for good. Whether things we are currently facing, or experiences from our past, God doesn't waste anything that we go through or learn in life.

All Things

It is also true, however, that the most difficult of experiences can be used for God and for good. One of the hardest passages of the Bible to live out is James 1:2-4: 'Count it all joy, my brothers, when you meet trials of various kinds, for you know that the testing of your faith produces steadfastness. And let steadfastness have its full effect, that you may be perfect and complete, lacking in nothing.' It's a great concept and is a perfect example of bad being used for good. The reality is far harder than the idea, especially if we are facing major grievances, loss, life-crippling diagnosis, debt or a relationship breakdown, or even, as was the case for many of the original readers, persecution. To think that God could work those things for our good and maybe even the good of others is hard to comprehend.

One of the things that makes this so difficult for those who love Jesus, is that it is extremely rare for us to notice or see that God is working a situation to our good at the time. When suffering surrounds us, when grief is raw, when things don't go the way we thought they should, it can often feel as though the opposite is true and that no good could possibly come of 'x'. This is why at the start of this chapter I mentioned hindsight. It is often only as we look back that we see that God has worked things together for our good. But it is in the difficult times that holding on to the truth of a verse such as this one from Romans becomes so important. This verse is a promise. It is a promise that has been formed from the experiences of a man who has been through so much suffering and been able to look back and see God's hand on his life. It's a promise that Paul witnesses to being fulfilled time and time again in the lives of others and as he travelled from place to place with the gospel, seeing the churches he loved facing persecution but still thriving and growing. It's a promise that Paul had seen in his own life. He knows that nothing in his life, even from when he was the 'worst of sinners' (see 1 Timothy 1:15), has been wasted and it has all been used by the God he is in relationship with, for good, so much good. We need to hold on to promises and testimonies like this in our challenging times, to remember these verses, because they testify to what we may not be able to see in the moment.

We need to recognise the role of the Spirit in this too. This kind of perseverance and the trust that is required to believe that God is working things to our good is something that we often cannot do alone. In Romans 5:1-5, Paul is preaching the same message as James about character-developing trust. Whereas James says we need wisdom to live this way, Paul says that it is the hope that is inside us, by the Holy Spirit, that gives us what we need to persevere through trial. It's the hope we spoke of previously, the unwavering certainty of us knowing we follow a God who knows what He is doing, even when we don't see it. In both James' and Paul's cases – there is a clear acknowledgement of the full reliance on God that is needed in order to hold fast to the truth that He is the one who is able to work things together for our good.

The whole biblical narrative, leading up to and including Jesus, also testifies to this promise:

The blessing of Jacob, despite his deception and all that followed with that family line.

The disobedience of Jonah and the personal journey of faith that God led him through and the salvation that followed for many.

The nation desiring a king, despite God advising them against it, that led to the rule of David – the royal line from which Jesus would ultimately be born.

David himself, who we know was far from perfect but, as we see from the Psalms, saw God working things together for his good.

Ultimately the cross, that first Good Friday – something that the human onlookers saw as failure, humiliation and finality – God turned around for the good of the whole of humanity.

Then Jesus' death was turned to a resurrection and life for all who live for the risen Jesus!

It could be argued that we see this promise being made by Jesus himself in the beatitudes. As he stands on the mount, Jesus is listing things that this world would see as struggles and pain – persecution, grief, mourning, poverty, meekness – but look at what is promised to those who experience these things: the kingdom of heaven, peace, blessing, seeing God. If this isn't God working all things together for the good of those who love Him, then I don't know what is!

When we are in difficult times, as individuals, as a community or even as a nation, we may not feel it, we may not see it, but we can stand on the promise that whatever we are facing will be worked together for our good. Maybe not right now, maybe not tomorrow, perhaps not even this year – but it will work out for our good. If something doesn't seem good, then it could be that God is still working that situation to be good and more time is needed. We don't have to feel something for it to be a truth. I urge you and encourage you to commit this verse from Romans to your memory, to add it to your arsenal when the doubts rise up – that whatever is happening, you have a tried and tested promise to stand on.

Do you Love me?

The important thing to note here, however, is that this verse is often misquoted, so when memorising it you will need to ensure you have the whole verse. It is very clear that God does work things together for good, but it is for the good of *those who love Him*. This isn't something that God just does for anybody, it is a privilege of being a son or daughter of God. So, the question we need to ask in difficult times is: 'Do I love Him?' This is the kind of love that is a choice not a feeling. Are you choosing to love God, even if it seems as though no good is coming your way?

At the time of writing, I have a friend and colleague who is having treatment for cancer. She is an inspiration to me because her desire for this time isn't necessarily for healing (though of course she would love to be healed); her main desire is that her relationship with Jesus grows stronger, deeper, more intimate than ever before. This is someone who is clearly in love with Jesus, despite the circumstances she is facing – so she seeks to recognise the 'good' when it happens. She can see (even if not always in the moment) when experiences are helping this to happen. She knows that being closer to Jesus is 'her good' at this moment in time. There may be other good that comes from it, but for now Jesus is enough, the relationship is enough, He is good enough. That is not to say that it is easy for her, but she has learnt to seek God rather than simply seeking healing. If you expect the healing to be the only 'good thing' God could do for you then you may miss all the other good He is working – all because He loves you and wants you to love Him. We grow in what we focus on. If we are only focusing on the negative and what we are not getting, that is what we will see. If, however, we are looking for the good, then the good is what we will find. It may feel like a treasure hunt at times, but the good is there to be found.

When you love somebody, and they love you in return, and want what is best for you, then it is easier to trust them and to trust that they know what they are doing. That kind of person becomes the person you want to be with and spend your time with, and they become the person that you are likely to want to have around you during the difficult times. Any good parent, for example, would want the best for their children – they would do anything to bring about good for them if they could. Sometimes, that parent will know things that the child doesn't about what is to come, and that parent will hopefully gain the child's love and trust because that child will know that they are loved. The child then, with knowledge of that love, wants to be with that parent, and chooses to in times of need. We need to ask ourselves if Jesus is that person to us. Is He the one we love and trust the most? Is He the one whom we would choose to have around us in the difficult times? Has He earned our trust? We, as children of God, can only 'love because He first loved us' (1 John 4:19), and that love always hopes, perseveres and trusts because it is a love that we know 'never fails' (1 Corinthians 13:7), because it is the love of a perfect father, who loves us and that love causes Him to do what is best for us, even if we don't see it at the time. Our love then, is a response to the love that we have received from Him, and what an outrageous love it is! His love alone should be good enough – any other good things that come our way are an added bonus, a blessing we don't deserve, from a father who loves to bless His children.

Good

We also need to be aware of the fact that God has a far better idea of what is good for us than we do. There have been many times, when I look back, that I have been glad that God didn't answer a prayer about something, which I may have deemed to be right or good for me. I can see the alternative that God provided has been far better for me in each and every case. I hate to think what my life might look like today if I was left entirely to my own devices, or if God always did things the way I expected or wanted Him to. God's understanding of good can be very different from ours.

This, for me, is made clear in the aforementioned passage from James chapter 1. Considering it joy in troubles because of what it leads to, is the key to understanding more of God's view of good. We would want to see suffering alleviated as soon as possible – but God can see a much larger picture than the one we see. He knows what we can handle, He knows how different we will be on the other side. He is wanting to make us into the best versions of ourselves that we could possibly be. One of the striking things about some of the stories of the wilderness times in the Bible is that the majority of the time, people are in the wilderness because God led them there (Exodus 13:18, Matthew 4:1). Does this mean that God leads us into suffering? That is a question we may never know the answer to this side of heaven. If He has led people into 'wilderness times' before, there is no reason why He wouldn't still be doing so now. Although, it could be said that His intention of doing so is not to lead us into suffering, but suffering is a reality of living in a fallen and broken world. Regardless of whether God leads us *to* those wilderness times, we can be sure that He does lead us and guide us *through* those places and seasons in our lives, as long as we are choosing to love Him, trust Him and follow Him, wherever. We can choose joy whatever we face, we can choose to love Him regardless, and when we do, He is leading us to places where we can become those better versions of ourselves when we come out the other side, and maybe even before we reach the other side. Joshua was a changed man before he reached the promised land, and the work that God had done in him was what made him one of only a few, of the original chosen ones, who still believed God would deliver on His promises. God is genuinely working things together for our good, even in the wilderness times. I have found in my own life, that the word 'good' doesn't seem to cut it. Looking back, I would say that God's plans, and the outcomes and changes in me that he has brought about, have far exceeded good.

An Added Benefit

Many people have tried to write books, blogs or sermons on suffering and on overcoming difficult times, or seeing the good from within them or from the other side of them. By far, however, the ones that are the most helpful, are the ones written by people who have lived through the pain, and in some cases are still living with the pain, hurt and struggles, but are finding ways to trust God in them. There is something powerful when God turns someone's struggles to bless others too. A few years ago, someone close to me experienced depression along with bulimia. It was a tough time. It was painful to have someone whom I loved, going through suffering, and not really knowing how to help. They had occasional glimpses of breakthrough, but it was a long and difficult journey. This person received counselling of various kinds, and prayer at every opportunity. She had great friends around her who were a good support, but although they and others helped her through, the pain was still very real.

Depression, as those who have suffered or are suffering from it will tell you, is not something that you ever get rid of, so it is still a reality in her life, but that person is blessing others with her beautiful honesty, vulnerability and realness, mainly through blog writing and sharing her story with others. She learnt, in that time, the importance of talking about what she was going through with friends and family as well as counsellors when needed. She learnt the importance (and power) of vulnerability. Now when she writes a blog post, or delivers a talk, God is using the pain she went through, not only for her good, but also for the good of others.

I have been personally blessed by people being very real about their struggles and by them sharing what God has revealed to them, or done in them and through them during those times. These stories can give us hope when we go through our own difficult times. They can remind us that the promise Paul speaks of in this verse (which by now I hope you have committed to memory) is backed up by real life examples, and probably from people you know, love, trust and respect, not just the book and blog writers. They are testament to the fact that God knows how to work all things to the good of those who love Him. And He is the same God for you today as He has been and is for them.

Lord, thank you that you truly do work all things together for my good. In times when it is hard to see this, remind me of your goodness. In the times I don't feel, or see your goodness, bring this truth to mind.

In times when I struggle to believe it to be true, surround me with people who can show me that it is.

Help me to grow more in love with you in the good times, so that in the hard times I will be able to trust that you are making me into the best version of myself that I can possibly be.

Thank you for where you have already worked, where you are working, and where you will work things together for my good, and by your grace, for the good of others. Amen!

11 FREEDOM

For the law of the Spirit of life has set you free.

-8:2-

Due to the fact that I am a vicar, as a family, we have had to move house a few times in recent years. The houses have been variable in size and design, but all a blessing to us, but there is something about having a larger garden that seems to make a huge difference. In one particular garden, we had to stop playing tennis when our son's power swing developed quicker than his accuracy with it – there simply wasn't enough space for him to develop his skills. In the same garden we had a small trampoline which would just about fit three of our children on it, but they had to bounce in a very organised and particular way in order to avoid collision.

When we moved to our current home, things changed – the garden is far larger, so our son can hit his tennis ball as hard as he likes in any direction and it would still be safely within our own space – no more need to ask the neighbours to throw our ball back every five minutes. There is room for a large enough trampoline for all four of our children – although collisions are inevitable, they happen far less. They can run, explore, climb, investigate and enjoy the space to their hearts' content. As a father, there is little I enjoy more than sitting out in the garden on a warm summer's day and just watching them enjoy the freedom that is provided by having more space, but space within the safety of clear boundaries. We were especially grateful of this space during the pandemic lockdowns and knew it be a blessing not to be taken for granted.

Free from What?

If we are to understand the freedom that we have as Christians, and the freedom that Paul speaks of here, we need, first, to know what it is that we are freed from. As has been said previously, Paul spends much of the opening chapters of Romans addressing and reminding the readers about this very thing. Just think for a moment where we would be without Christ. Think about what your future would be. Reflect on what you would deserve for the wrong that you have done, for your rebellion against God. Jesus, as well as being our friend, has also set us free from so much of what we deserve. In fact, 'He laid down His life' for us (John 15:13) in order to make this possible. There is a powerful freedom that is found at the cross of Jesus Christ. A freedom won for us by grace.

I find that the concept of God's grace only makes sense in the context of God's wrath and judgement – two themes that people are not often comfortable with. But if we really want to grasp a fuller understanding of grace and of what we have been freed from, then we need to have a greater understanding, and even acceptance, of the judgement and wrath of God.

God is a God who is perfect, and just, and righteous. Such a God could not simply allow sin and disobedience to go unpunished. If He was to turn a blind eye to these things, or expect or demand no recompense, then surely, He wouldn't be *fully* just. If He allowed people to get away with anything, with no consequence, or if He only let one thing go unpunished, then surely, He would not be *fully* righteous.

Like it or not, our rebellion against God, our need to be in control and to have it all our own way, isn't what God intended for us. Our desires (deliberate or not) to completely ignore God's ways, must have consequences, and those consequences require discipline. In the same way that any parent who loves their children sets clear boundaries and expects to issue consequences when those boundaries are challenged or even broken, so God, as a perfect father, needs to show that there are consequences to us doing so to Him and His boundaries.

We need discipline. We deserve to experience the wrath of God. These are not nice words to read or to hear, but they are a truth about God and His justice that we can't ignore. The gospel, in many ways, is offensive because it tells us that we are all natural-born sinners, that we deserve punishment for our sin, that we can't save ourselves and that we need someone to save us from ourselves.

Then, from stage left, completely unexpected and entirely undeserved, enters the grace of God. The grace of God that moved Him to take that punishment and to face the wrath on our behalf, to be, what the Book of Common Prayer states as the 'propitiation (atonement, offering) for our sins' (see also 1 John 2:2). The grace of God worked in perfect unity in and through the Trinity to break the wall that separated us from God, the wall that otherwise would have been our demise and destruction as we stood face to face with a perfect God. The temple curtain was violently torn in two during the crucifixion (Matthew 27:51, Mark 15:38), granting us full access to God, and grace flooded the world. And so, in that moment, a way was made for the repentant heart to turn to Jesus, the only way to the Father (John 14:6), to accept what He has done for us, to find forgiveness of sin and be saved from the judgement that sin deserves

– causing us, as Paul puts it in verse 1 of Romans 8 (as explored in chapter 1 of this book), to be free from condemnation. What amazing grace!

Paul makes it clear, however, that the Spirit has a part to play here too. It is the Spirit of God who convicts us of our need for Jesus in the first place: 'And when He [the Holy Spirit] comes, He will convict the world concerning sin and righteousness and judgement' (John 16:8). It is He who leads us to the cross, who brings us to the point of surrender. It is the Spirit who opens our eyes to this radical grace, as He Himself is the 'Spirit of Grace' (see Hebrews 10:29), who shows us what we are saved from. It is He who meets us in that place of brokenness and rebellion, lifts us up and moves us on. It is the Spirit who then goes on to raise Jesus from the dead, adding to the freedom from sin, freedom from death which was the symptom of that sin (Genesis 3:19). It is the same Spirit who seals our relationship with Jesus and then goes on to be all that Jesus promised He would be; the counsellor, the comforter, the gift giver, all for the sake of our freedom. It is the same Spirit who seals our identity, who woos us daily into a closer, more intimate relationship with the Father. And so yes, the Spirit has set us free, and is setting us free!

There is also another freedom – we are freed from the Old Testament sacrificial system that had previously been required in order for people in God's community to be right with God. Part of God's requirement for people in order to understand the severity of their sin, was to sacrifice things as a sign of repentance. In 21st-century England, I find it hard to imagine what it would have been like to witness or be part of animal sacrifices, and to have them as the primary method for atoning my sin and wrongdoing. The closest I have come was during my first degree when our lecturer in Old Testament texts re-enacted an animal sacrifice using an overhead projector and a teddy bear! But despite not having experienced genuine sacrifice, my imagination does allow me to form enough of a picture of what it may have been like. It is enough of a picture to cause me to be thankful that I don't have to do it – particularly as I am a priest. The more I read about the Old Testament sacrificial system, the more thankful I am for Jesus becoming the one true sacrificial lamb (see 1 Peter 1:18-19), and paying the price for us, freeing us from this form of atonement.

It is important to note, however, that being free from the sacrificial system does not excuse us from sacrifice altogether. Although the sacrifice we offer may require a little less bloodshed, it is by no means easier. When presenting offerings to be sacrificed, the Jewish people were not required to just offer the first animal they laid hands on, they were expected to offer the best of the best – the animal that could have fetched the highest price at market, could have produced the best offspring, could have graced the finest table – this was the kind of sacrifice God desired (or the nearest equivalent, depending on your financial status). We too, are called to offer the best of the best, but in terms of our entire lives. Paul states in Romans 12 that we are to 'offer our bodies as living sacrifices, Holy and pleasing to God' (Romans 12:1-2). A life of worship, surrendered to the will of God. There has, however, been a significant shift because of what Jesus has done for us on the cross. The purpose of the sacrifice in the Old Testament was to show a desire for forgiveness, to make a person's relationship with God right again. For us, as people who have been saved by the one true sacrifice and been made clean by His blood, we offer ourselves as living sacrifices in *response* to what God has done for us. The truth is that He has always been worthy of sacrifice, and always will be. We are free from the sacrificial system of old, but not free from sacrifice; it is a sacrifice we gladly offer, although hard at times, in response to His love for us and His sacrifice for us. In fact, as we offer this sacrifice and share in His sufferings, then we are sharing God's glory.

In the church calendar of some traditions, the season of Lent provides a good opportunity to reflect on all of this, and gives us a way to grow in our appreciation for all that Jesus went on to do for us in that first Holy Week. Whilst not all traditions recognise Lent in this way, it is good for us to take times, whether through private or led reflection, to remind ourselves often of the price that Jesus paid for us on the cross, and of the sacrifices He made for us.

Free and Protected

Have you ever played a game where there are no rules? A football match with no referee? When there is no-one to encourage proper rule keeping in the game, it may seem fun and freeing at first, but it isn't long before things start to change. Most likely, the time you will notice it most is when someone tackles you unfairly and there is no-one there to hold them to account. There is no-one to punish them for the wrong they did to you. You know full well that if a referee had been there, this vicious tackler would have been booked, warned, maybe even sent off the pitch – but as there is no referee, and no rules, the sense of injustice just grows within you. It may even be that you feel the need to take matters into you own hands if the opportunity were to present itself. Ten minutes later you find yourself sliding in with two feet, thinking, 'well if he can get away with it then so can I!' It sounds barbaric doesn't it? That desire to take matters into our hands is part of our natural, fallen human state, and is evidence that there is a natural state of rebellion in us. But in order for there to be rebellion there needs to be something that we are rebelling against. This rebellion is on show throughout scripture. It was evident not long after the Fall, when Cain murdered Abel because he thought that God wasn't doing His job properly or fairly enough (Genesis 4). We see it when the people of Israel demand a king in order to be like other nations and have someone 'rule over them' (1 Samuel 8). We see it when Abraham sleeps with Hagar to hurry along the process of having his firstborn (Genesis 16). All of these are obvious examples of rebellion, but they are a rebellion against parameters, or guidelines, set by God. It is not as if, like the rule-less football match, that there no rules to rebel against, and no-one to hold us account.

I wonder, therefore, if the giving of the commandments, the parameters around which our fallen, human nature is called to live, is actually one of the greatest pieces of evidence to show that we have a God who has a desire for justice and freedom – but that true freedom is actually found within parameters. I believe that God knows that if left to our own devices, when we try to do things our own way, when we have nothing to hold justice up against, things won't go as well as they would if we followed the ways of the God who has our best interests at heart.

As well as this, I believe that these rules, that we have in the ten commandments, actually enable us to live more in freedom than life without them would. It is a freedom we can enjoy with a knowledge of protection, with an understanding of right and wrong, just and unjust. God knows, more than anyone, what harms us, what would harm other people, and His desire is to protect us and others from those things, as any father would his own children:

'I want you to know that I am your Dad, and no-one else could be.'

'I am keen to make sure that nothing becomes more important to you than our connection with one another.'

'Please respect my name and our family name.'

'Let's have a day together. I'll take time off work, you can have a day off homework, and we will focus on investing in our relationship. It would be great to do this as often as possible so that we don't lose our connection.'

I don't think these would be unreasonable requests from any father, and this is essentially what God says in the commandments. The other commandments about not murdering, stealing and coveting are clearly not only for the good and protection of others but are also for our own good. We know that these things are not good for us – so it makes sense that God would want to protect us from the harm that they would cause and He does so by making them things that are completely off limits when it comes to living for Him. Much of our legal justice system is based on these commandments and few of us would disagree that this is a good thing.

It may not always be easy to keep these commandments, for example it can be hard to honour parents who have never honoured us, but it can help to remember that these commands are not given to be a killjoy, or to rob us of anything, or to make life impossible for us. They are given to help us, protect us and bring the best out of us. God's desire is still that His people are a holy people (see 1 Peter 1:16), as was His desire with Israel. If holiness means to be set apart, to be different from world, then these commandments are a basic understanding of this holiness or a guideline for it. They are a bottom line, non-negotiable standard for people who have a desire to live differently. But God knew that these laws, although important for our safety, would not be enough alone to save us. We would always rebel against them because in our natural state we find the concept of surrender so hard. He knew that to save us, He had to do something to show His love even more than these commandments do, but in so doing, through Jesus, He also showed that it is possible to live by these rules and that we don't miss out on life if we do; in fact we gain life.

Seeing that these rules actually enhance our freedom is one of the things that sets us apart. I love how the psalmists often write about 'loving God's laws' just a quick glance through Psalm 119, for example, will show that those who truly loved God saw the commandments as a gift not a burden. We are free to be who we were meant to be and created to be, because of and through what Jesus has done for us. We are free to be in relationship with God, the relationship as God always intended it to be. And because of the commandments that God has set for us, we are simultaneously free and protected within those boundaries – like a child in a securely fenced garden, under the watchful and loving eye of their father.

It is for Freedom

One question that people have often asked me about freedom is 'why did God set us free?' Well in one short answer we could say that it was because of His great love for us as His people. It is His desire, as it has always been, that we live in freedom. He desires for us to be free from shame, free from guilt, free from the bonds that hold us back from true relationship with our perfect heavenly father. This is how He originally designed it to be, and He has made a way for it to be like that again.

We were all once bound by our circumstances, trapped in our own sin, hemmed in by our own guilt and shame. The difference is that we have always been in a 'large garden' but, like a dog tied to a stake in the ground, we were not free to enjoy it. We have bound ourselves by choosing to live in rebellion, and not in the life that God had intended for us. This is why God sent Jesus, because He never intended us to live that way. He wants us to have and to enjoy freedom, to enjoy what He has given us within the safety of the boundaries that He has set. We can't just do whatever we like and get away with it, but we can enjoy a freedom of relationship like never before – Jesus removed the stake that we put there ourselves through our own rebellion, and with the stake removed, we can be free.

There is, however, a choice we still have: to step into and enjoy that freedom. The alternative is to add new ties or restrictions through becoming more 'religious'. Often, we can partly accept the freedom but hold on to some shame, or unforgiveness, or other things that Jesus came to remove. We can be like someone who walks into the most amazing theme park but doesn't get on any rides,[11] or the person who walks into an all-you-can-eat buffet with foods from around the world, and just eats the chips. When we hold on to our guilt and our shame, it can undermine the very thing that Jesus came to die for – our freedom from such things. And so, Paul is able to say, unapologetically, in one of his other letters, it is 'for freedom that Christ has set us free' (Galatians 5:1). God doesn't need any other reason than that. If He wants to set us free for freedom's sake then He can do that. We need to ask then: do we feel free? Are we enjoying the freedom He won for us? Are we so concerned with rules and religion (more than just the ten commandments) that we fail to enjoy the relationship? Do we hold on to our past, our shame and our, already forgiven, sin so tightly that we refuse to let God show us how free He wants us to be?

How to Experience Freedom

All this freedom sounds like a nice idea, but some may be asking how we experience it, how we accept it, walk in it, live in it in our own lives? It involves a simple but powerful word: yes. God's Holy Spirit does not force Himself on anyone, and He doesn't force people into freedom, otherwise it would be obligation. He doesn't command you to accept the freedom He offers, because He wants it to be your choice. What God wants from us is our 'yes'. Our 'yes' to accepting the gift of freedom that He offers by His Spirit. Our 'yes' to surrendering the part(s) of us that we have tried (unsuccessfully) to control for so long. Our 'yes' to trusting the fact that what He has for us will be far greater than anything we could lose. Our 'yes' to remembering daily the fact that it is grace and grace alone that can set us free – a gift we can receive. True freedom is actually found in surrendering to our need of God, to depend on Him for all things.

Secondly, we give God our time. When we surrender our lives to Jesus, He deposits something of Himself in us, in fact His full self is in us (as we have previously explored), but we want to grow our relationship with Christ more and more each and every day, to nurture what is within. We don't nurture our relationship in the same way you would a plant where you are responsible for watering it, replanting it when it grows, making sure it has all it needs, but rather it is more like nurturing yeast in a bread mix – you put it in the right environment and allow the process to happen naturally, and the right environment in this case is the presence of God. That means we take time to put ourselves intentionally into God's presence, to spend time in worship and prayer and reading His word. Time with an attitude of thankfulness, fellowship, community, stillness and having quality time with God, so that by His Spirit He can help develop and grow us to be more and more like Christ and to experience more and more of the freedom that comes with that. We are always in God's presence, but we need times where we intentionally increase our awareness of Him with us and in us.

The fruits of the Spirit will then become a natural symptom of someone who is placing themselves into the presence of God on a regular basis and from that place becoming free to be the best version of the themselves, as they take on more and more of the family resemblance of their perfect heavenly Father, becoming more like Christ (1 Corinthians 11:1, 2 Corinthians 3:17-18, 1 John 2:6). All of this is possible because freedom isn't found in process, ritual, tasks, religion or to do lists. True freedom is found in relationship with the Trinity, and being surrendered to that relationship. When we take time to invest in that relationship we grow in our understanding and acceptance of that freedom.

Are you free? Are you experiencing the freedom that God has always intended for you to have? Before you read any more of this book, is there any way you can make more time for God, right now? Are you prepared to give God your 'yes'?

Lord, thank you that you came that I may be free. Forgive me for any times I have taken that freedom for granted. Help me today to claim and step into the freedom that you have won for me. I surrender to your Holy Spirit and ask you to show me freedom from sin, freedom from shame, freedom from guilt and freedom to be all that you have called me to be. I give you my 'yes' and choose to give you my time. Amen!

12 TEMPLES

You, however, are not in the flesh but in the Spirit, if in fact the Spirit of God dwells in you.

-8:9-

I love the Holy Spirit. It dawned on me recently that this isn't a phrase we hear much in Church. One thing that I have realised over the years is that churches have very different views on the work and person of the Holy Spirit. I remember, as a very young Christian, leading a Christian Union in my school. To feed my own curiosity and desire to know more about the Holy Spirit, I decided to lead a session on that subject. The session seemed to go well and provoked some good discussion, some of which helped me to understand, some of it muddied the waters a little more. The comment that stayed with me, however, was one that was made after the session had ended. The Christian teacher who would always sit in on our sessions, but deliberately not contribute (unless we were close to heresy) approached me afterwards and said, "You need to remember that the Holy Spirit is a *He* not an *it*." I had unknowingly been referring to the Holy Spirit as an 'it' for the whole session because I knew no different. I had seen the Holy Spirt, up to that point, as a purely functional part of the Trinity, as more of a 'thing' than a person. After this kindly and gently-made correction, I began to look more into *who* the Holy Spirit is and what it was that He does *in* us and *through* us, as well as *for* us.

Not long after this, I did an Alpha course at my local church, and on the Holy Spirit away day, things began to make more sense to me. As we learned about the Spirit through teaching, I began to understand more about Him, but the real difference was when I experienced Him personally in a way that I never had before. It was as if my eyes were opened to what He was already doing and had been doing in my life – but more than that, I was learning who He was. I began to realise that I had a relationship with Him. When I led an Alpha course in my curacy church, a man in his 70s had a similar experience. He said to me after being prayed for:

'I have never understood the Holy Spirit before. In all my years coming to church I have had faith in God and a relationship with Jesus, but I have never been able to get my head around the Holy Spirit, even though you and others have taught about Him in church. Today though, when I was prayed for, I began to see moments in my life where the Holy Spirit had been at work, building my relationship with God, and I was able to say "Oh! that was Him, and that was Him…Oh! and He caused that…He revealed that to me." I began to see that He has been in my life since the moment I came to faith. I have been in relationship with Him without even knowing it.'

As you can imagine, this testimony made my heart sing. He was of course right, and this concept of the Holy Spirit living in us, dwelling in us, is what Paul is getting at in this verse. When we have the Spirit of God in us, our lives are transformed – even if we don't have the spiritual maturity, or often the language, to acknowledge that it is the Holy Spirit at the time. He is at work in us, making us more like Christ, sealing our identity, giving us revelation after revelation so that we can grow in our understanding of God. There are times He shows us things that need to change in us, or He reveals scripture to us at a time we need it. He teaches us right from wrong, He gifts us, equips us, woos us, calls us, encourages us, strengthens us, teaches us and grows us. He is doing within us, and for us, all the things that Jesus did for His disciples when He was on earth.

The Holy Spirit is not some optional tag-on of the Trinity; He is an essential part of the Godhead three-in-one. We can't just pick and choose whether to include Him in our lives or churches if our 'theology allows us to'! He is just as important as the Father and the Son to our life and faith. It makes me so sad now when I go to churches, or meet individuals, who either don't acknowledge the Spirit at all, or who perhaps do acknowledge Him but see Him (as I used to) as entirely functional. I don't judge them, or feel that they have got it all wrong, I just feel that they are missing out on something special and crucial. The Holy Spirit is promised in Joel 2:28 and we are reminded in Acts 2:17, that He is for *all* people.

I have come to realise also, that no-one knows me better than the Holy Spirit does. He knows what I need, what I can cope with, what I am feeling, thinking, experiencing – it is no coincidence that Jesus refers to Him the way that He does: 'When the counsellor comes, whom I will send to you from the Father, the Spirit of truth who goes out from the Father' (John 15:26 - NIV). He is also referred to as an 'advocate' (1 John 2:1), 'helper' (John 16:7) and 'teacher' (1 John 2:27). Looking back over my life at the people who have comforted, helped and taught me, the ones who have done this the best are the ones who took time to get to know me, to know my personality, my life experiences, my faith journey and my current situations. They would then take all those things into consideration when offering support or advice. The Holy Spirit knows me better than anyone else, so no-one is more equipped to be those things to me than He is. The reality is that if we choose to treat the Holy Spirit as purely functional then we are missing out on a relationship with the one person who knows us far better and more intimately than anyone else. If you have welcomed Him to do so, then He is already living in you, but how much do you acknowledge Him in your life?

I have noticed that those who treat the Holy Spirit as purely functional somehow don't seem to be as free – they appear (without wishing to come across as judgemental) to be striving for God's acceptance and approval all the time and they seem to feel as if they have to do all the work. They appear to be more like the older son of the prodigal son story. What some Christians can sometimes fail to realise is that because of all the work that Jesus has done on the cross, and because of the resurrection, and because of the gift of the Holy Spirit, we are accepted as His, and He chooses to dwell in us. That initial decision of repentance, that choice to follow Jesus and to want to walk in His ways was enough. We can have relationship with God and we become heirs of the Kingdom, and are entrusted with the joy of being temples to the Holy Spirit (1 Corinthians 6:19). God knows we cannot live the Christian life, or even truly live at all, without Him, yet so many are trying to do so. Sanctification (being made new) is a work of the Holy Spirit. Yes, we have disciplines in life that can help us, but we can't possibly expect to be more like Christ if we deny or don't accept what He has given us to help with this process.

Positive Possession

The word 'possession' or 'to be possessed' can sometimes have very negative connotations. We tend to think of films like *The Exorcist* or the effects that witchcraft or the occult can have. We tend to use 'possession' as a negative expression to explain something bad, but why? How would you feel, for example, about praying the words 'Lord, possess me with your Spirit?' What would that look like? Is that what we are asking for when we ask to be filled by the Spirit? If to be possessed means to be owned by another force then surely this can be a good thing, so long as we are possessed by God.

For some, the whole concept of having the Spirit of God dwell in them feels a little daunting. They may wonder 'what if He makes me do something I don't want to do?', 'what if He reveals that part of my past that I'm not willing to deal with?', what if He makes me a 'crazy' Christian?' Well, let me tell you, from my experience, He is completely trustworthy because He knows you better than you even know yourself. If you can trust the Father, then you can also trust the Spirit, but that doesn't mean He won't occasionally surprise you.

When I was going through the application process for ministry I had a very difficult season in my walk with God. I had always been someone who relied a great deal on my feelings, on 'feeling' that God was close – but for some reason, in this time I felt absolutely nothing. No matter how much I prayed, or read the Bible, or sang out in worship, I was feeling nothing. I decided in this time, that I would keep doing those things; keep praying, keep worshipping and keep reading, and trust that God knew what He was doing and that He was there, even though I couldn't *feel* His presence. After a while of this I asked God when it would end, and I had a date come to my mind. It was a date that I would never forget.

When the date came around, I was leading a camp for 16-18-year-olds. I had, despite my dryness and lack of feeling, been leading worship and speaking for the first part of the week before we reached the date in question. That evening, I was speaking (I can't quite remember what the subject was) but halfway through the talk I sensed a call to share honestly with the young people about what I had been going through – so I did, and as I did the tears began to fall. I shared with the young people that I thought that this 'dry phase' as I had named it, was due to come to an end that evening. I led a time of response and saw *all* of the young people respond. That was moving enough, but then I picked up my guitar to lead a song of response and I was suddenly surrounded by a group of young people who began to pray for me. The floodgates were truly opened – I wept like a baby (it really wasn't pretty) for over an hour. Then the unthinkable happened, I began to jerk a little – not a lot, but enough to remind me of something I had prayed during my 'dry phrase'. The prayer went a little something like this: 'God I want more of your Spirit, I want to feel you again in my life. I just don't want any of that 'crazy stuff' to happen. Lord I ask that when your Spirit fills me again that I won't weep and I won't jerk like those "crazy charismatic Christian" people do – I just want to know you are with me.'

Why do I share this? Well, because ever since that day, when the Spirit is moving either in my life, or in a time of gathered worship, I either weep or jerk (sometimes both). There are times when I am preaching and will begin to sob (again, not pretty). It was the last thing I wanted, but do I mind? No! I do not. I got what I asked for – to know that God is in my life, to know He is close. What I thought I didn't want, the Holy Spirit (who knows me better than I even know myself) knew what He wanted to give me. Why? I don't fully know, but I know that it is good, and I am thankful that I didn't get my own way because when these things happen I know He is close, that He is at work in me, because they are not things that I would humanly choose to do. There were probably some lessons for me to learn about surrender, about trusting God whatever happens. There may even be hints at God's sense of humour! But whatever the reason(s), I know that He knows me better than I do. He knows what I can cope with, what I need, what would help me to feel closer and to know when He is at work. I love Him and trust Him all the more for that.

If you are someone who is worried about inviting the Holy Spirit to work within you, I can't promise that He won't make you do something that *you* don't want to do. I can't promise that He won't reveal things that you need to deal with – but I can promise, through experience and through scripture, that whatever He has for you, it will be good (see Matthew 7:9-11).

He is the source of holiness and power, to be honoured and reverently adored. He is, at times, unpredictable, but we can know that whilst He might surprise you, and challenge your perceptions of Him, He would never do anything to harm you. We cannot put Him in a box, or guarantee or predict how He will work. He may call us to something amazing, outrageous. He may change us, shape us, mould us, challenge us, convict us, inspire us. He may call us to forgiveness, remind us of things we have not yet dealt with, that hinder our relationship with the Father. From these points of view, He is not safe, but He is good and He knows us intimately better than anyone else ever has or ever will, So I say: let Him do what He wants to do – you may even have some fun together along the way. Let Him possess you.

Same Power

In verse 11, Paul takes this thought even further when he says, 'If the Spirit of Him who raised Jesus from the dead dwells in you, He who raised Christ Jesus from the dead will also give life to your mortal bodies through His Spirit who dwells in you.' This, for me, is one of the most incredible concepts in scripture. The same power?! Is that really what Paul means? Well, yes! It is clearly what Paul means because He doesn't only say it here. He refers to this same power when he prays for the church in Ephesus, that they may know 'His incomparably great power for us who believe' (Ephesians 1:19 - NIV). A power that in verse 17, he acknowledges has been given to the Church. He also refers to this power when he prays, in Philippians 1:9-11, for the church to be filled so that they may be fruitful.

These statements from Paul make it clear that there is not a junior or apprentice version of the Holy Spirit for us. It is not that there is one Spirit for Jesus and another one for us. No, this is very much the same Spirit. I wonder whether that makes you feel any different about how you treat your body, for example, which Paul describes as a temple to the Holy Spirit (1 Corinthians 6:19). I wonder if it makes any difference to how you view what is possible when the two of you work together, what God can do in and through you? As those who have freely received this power and this presence, are we freely giving it to those who need him most (Matthew 10:8)?

Just think for a moment what kind of power it would have taken to raise a man from the dead. Let's not underestimate this. It wasn't some simple magic trick or illusion that happened on that first Easter day. No! When Jesus rose from the dead there was a power at work, a power so strong (which also happens to be the same power involved in creation) that it breathed life back into a dead and battered body, a body that been dead for three days. It was a power so strong that it moved a massive stone from a tomb to allow the risen Jesus to walk free. This is the power that defeated death. This is the power that breathes life into dry bones – and this power lives in you and me!

But as well as being powerful, He is also gentle and respectful. It is, after all, the same power that rested on Jesus as a dove at His baptism (Luke 3:22). As well as being 'unsafe' and 'unpredictable', He is also trustworthy and good. As well as knowing everything about you, He will be patient with you. He is not the uninvited guest who will do whatever He wants, whenever He wants, at least not without your approval to do so. He won't force Himself upon you. To be filled with the Spirit requires a conscious decision on our part – an invitation that says, 'Yes, I want this power within me', not so that I can become greater but because I know I need Him.

Do you want Him? Do you trust Him? The absolute reality is that you need Him, so why on earth would you want to try and live life without Him?

Father God, thank you for the gift of your Holy Spirit. Thank you that you sent Him to be for us what Jesus was to His disciples. I acknowledge my need for more of Him in my life today.

Holy Spirit, I ask you to fill me afresh, to possess me. As I receive you into my life, as the same power that raised Jesus from the dead, I ask you to make me more like Him.

I welcome you into my life, and I trust you to have your way with me, trusting that you know me better than I know myself. Come, Holy Spirit. Amen!

13 GROANS TOO DEEP FOR WORDS

The Spirit Himself intercedes for us with groanings too deep for words.

-8:26-

Headlines can be funny things. There can be some headlines that draw us into the stories that end up being far less exciting than the headline suggested, particularly in local news. There are headlines that are so clever in how they play on words, that you can imagine teams of people sitting round a board room table coming up with them. One of my particular favourites was a football related one I saw a number of years ago. I can't remember what paper it was from, but even though I am not hugely into football or profess to know much about it, I remember seeing this headline in a newsagent and had to admire the genius behind it. The story was that one lower ranked football team in the Scottish league beat a team that should have won easily. The headline simply read:

Super Caley go ballistic, Celtic are atrocious![12]

I wish headlines could always be that fun, but often the opposite is true. The headlines we read today, far too often, are not designed to put a smile on our face, or make us think how clever the editors are at funny word play. Many headlines we read can shock us, surprise us, upset us, and even anger us.

'In the News Today...'

There is no denying that sometimes life hurts. We may go through some suffering ourselves or, as can sometimes be harder, we can witness someone close to us suffer. It is hard to experience and hard to live with. But even if our own life is comfortable and safe, we are surrounded by suffering.

In recent times, it can be hard to be at home watching the news without feeling very sad about what is going on around this broken world. As we hear about another attack, in another city, or read of more corruption in leadership, or wrong decisions being made around the world. We can hear or read horrific stories of how one human being treats or mistreats another, purely because of the colour of their skin, or the origin of their birth, and sometimes for no given reason at all, and all we can do it sit in silence – not knowing how to respond. 2020 was a year like no other, as the world faced a global pandemic that rendered many of us speechless by its sheer scale and lasting effects, that we may be experiencing for many years to come. There were many times during that pandemic when I, and many others, simply didn't know what to pray.

In times like this we may pray, asking God to alleviate the suffering. We may ask others to pray – but I find that the longer the suffering continues, the harder it becomes to pray, or at least to know what to pray. It can feel like the prayers have, seemingly to this point, gone unanswered and, although we may know the truth of Romans 8:28 referred to in chapter 10, it can be hard to see it. On one level we may feel that our prayers are going unheard by God, but I wonder if our prayers 'stop working' for us long before they 'stop working' for God. What I mean by this, is that the prayers can easily become routine. We can pray without thinking or feeling anything, we can become numb as we pray, we can feel as though we are just going through the motions because we feel we 'ought' to pray. We may believe on an intellectual level that prayer changes things, but the longer the suffering continues, the harder it can become to really believe this biblical and experiential truth. We can also lose sight of who we are praying to. The danger then becomes that we can also face a subconscious decision – to stop praying altogether about that situation (although we may still ask others to pray on our behalf, hoping that their prayers will have more success). There is a second option, however, and that is to move into intercession.

When we move into intercession there is a shift in our thinking, in the way we approach prayer. I think the difference between prayer and intercession is the focus of our attention. In prayer, we will be focused on what we want to see happen, the hoped-for outcome of our prayers. In intercession, however, our focus is on who we are praying to and who can make that change happen – God, and God alone. It is when we enter into this realm of intercessory prayer that we recognise, discover, or at least remember, that words are not the most important part of our prayers. This prayer is no longer an item on a 'prayer shopping list' but something we cry out to God for, believing that change is possible because we are praying to God. A determination seems to set in that I believe to be a Spirit-fuelled determination.

The reality is still, however, that sometimes a situation will move us to a point where we simply don't have the words, or that it feels like words will mean nothing. In these moments, we are moved, either to complete silence (which is just as much a form of prayer as anything else) or simply to cry, groan or even wail.

'Too British' to Wail

A number of years ago, I was called by the family of man who was in the final stages of a fight against cancer. In his final days he was reaching out to God and so he wanted to talk to someone from the church about this faith that he was discovering. He was finding a peace and solace in prayer, the likeness of which he had never experienced anywhere else before, which seemed odd to him considering the circumstances around him. He knew he only had weeks to live, he was weak, his passion of playing music had been taken away from him as he was getting weaker and weaker. He was grieving, not necessarily at the thought of his death, but of what and who he would be leaving behind. He was seeing his family suffer, he was surrounded by carers, he was taking huge amounts of medication just to remain pain free, he was confined to his bed – yet even with all of this, when his Christian friends from work came to visit him and prayed for him, he experienced this perfect peace. The 'peace which surpasses all understanding' (Philippians 4:7).

A few weeks later he passed away, peacefully and in love with Jesus. It was huge privilege to minister in this situation. I found it hard to know what to pray at this time. I was torn by wanting to pray for full and total healing and also feeling as though I should be praying for peace. It was even harder, however, to know how to pray for his family, who didn't share his newly discovered faith. All I could pray was that they would know what he had come to know about Jesus.

But I also learnt something very significant about prayer and grief during this time. It was few months after his passing that I went to visit his widow. It was clear that grief was having a huge impact on her life; she was receiving help for this, which I was pleased to discover, but she said these words to me: "I want to go to church but I find it hard being in public places because there are times that all I want to do is wail, to really let go and wail, and I don't think that would be appropriate in church."

I found myself thinking – why not? Why would wailing be inappropriate in church? I began to imagine how that would play out in our church, if on a Sunday morning, we were there in our nice comfortable middle-class church, with its reserved middle-class people, and in verse three of the opening song someone begins to wail uncontrollably. How would people react? How would they cope with the 'disruption'?

When we look at scripture, however, we see that wailing can be one of the most profound and deepest forms of intercession. What is wailing if not our spirits crying out to the God who knows us, who knows what we are experiencing, who understands the grief that sometimes we can't even find the words to describe. I believe that even if the person in grief doesn't acknowledge that they are crying to God, their tears are not going unnoticed by Him.

Consider for a moment Jesus looking out over Jerusalem in Luke 19:41-44. In this moment the words don't cut it, so He simply (yet profoundly) weeps. Those tears could be more prayerful than any words He could have used in that moment as He reflected on both the history and the current state of His children and their state, and as He began to focus on what was required of Him to save them. The same is true when Jesus learns of the death of his good friend Lazarus (see John 11:35).

This deep wailing, weeping, intercessory prayer, when words fail us and emotion takes over, is one possible way of understanding Paul's use of the expression of 'groans too deep for words', but there is another possible interpretation.

Tongues

I had been a Christian for a short while and was still fairly new to the whole prayer thing. I was at a weekend conference, and during the second evening meeting the teaching was on prayer. The person on the platform began to teach about praying in tongues. I can't remember all the details of what was being said, but I can distinctly remember feeling hugely inadequate as I received the message from what he was saying as being 'prayer is not really prayer unless you pray in tongues'.

I had heard people pray in tongues before (the first time I did I was completely freaked out), and I had many friends who prayed in tongues, and I had grown over the years to be slightly less concerned by it, but I had never prayed in tongues myself, nor really had any desire to do so. But as I heard this message I felt rubbish. I believed (the lie) that all my prayers up to that point had meant nothing to God as I wasn't speaking 'His language'. The sad thing is that I have known a number of people walk away from church altogether because of teaching like this. I think had I been in a church at the time, I may very well have just walked out and never gone back, but as I was on a retreat in the middle of nowhere that wasn't an option, and I am very thankful that God had a different plan for me.

I moved myself to the back of the venue and slumped myself down against a wall. As the speaker led a time of prayer ministry, I zoned out from what was happening around me and began to wallow in my own self-pity. I was vaguely aware that some amazing things were happening in the venue, but I could not shake the feeling that I had of my prayers being 'rubbish'. Then I began to cry, just one or two tears, but I could feel the emotion rising up from within me. This wasn't the Holy Spirit as I have experienced since then (see previous chapter); it was just grief. Grief at my prayer life being rubbished. But then I just said the word 'Daddy' and then I began to weep as I heard a voice (I am assuming it was God) gently say, "that's all I need to hear." He instantly, in that moment, restored and reinstated everything that had been robbed of me by the teaching that the enemy had twisted into a horrendous lie that almost destroyed my fairly new relationship with God. I didn't say a single word in tongues, in fact I only said a single word (and shed lots of tears), but in that moment I realised, more than ever before, that prayer is about relationship, not about the words; and my relationship was deepened with a single cry.

Since then, I have prayed, and now often do, pray in tongues, and looking back it could be that I may not have fully understood what the preacher was trying to say. (I am not sure if that is because I was young, or because how he delivered his teaching left him open to misinterpretation, or whether he did just do some bad teaching.) I do now believe that praying in tongues is a great gift, but I do still firmly believe that not praying in tongues does not make you any less of a Christian, it does not make your prayer any less valuable to God. It is not as though there are two classes of Christian, those who pray in tongues and those who do not. In my own experience there have been times when I don't have the words to say, and when I pray in tongues, although I don't know what I am praying, I believe I am praying and that what I am praying has a significance about it that my own words may not have. I am in those moments, I believe, praying with groans too deep for words.

Teaching on this subject, as I have experienced, sadly has the ability to divide churches. People can either shut themselves off entirely from the idea of praying in tongues (as I did for some time after that conference), or they can believe that praying in tongues is the be all and end all of prayer. I believe, however, there to be a middle ground that says that tongues are a gift to us (as Paul describes them to be); indeed they are a gift to be 'eagerly desired' (see 1 Corinthians 12:31). They are, however, not necessarily a gift for our benefit, but they can do something to our prayer life that can help us to connect with God when we do not have the words.

Sometimes, these tongues, or other languages, sound like groans, but I don't believe that Paul is talking about an audible sound in this verse, but rather to a reality of an action of groaning, crying, calling out, weeping, wailing – that ultimately is about connecting with God in a way that words are not able to. This is about deep crying out to deep. In Psalm 42:7 the writer is talking about how suffering comes after suffering and he gives the example of two overpowering waterfalls side by side. I have found that this phrase can also be used to describe something of the connection between us and God when that suffering comes. In these times of groaning intercession, it can feel as though the deepest part of us (our soul, our will) is crying out to the deepest part of God.

Spirit Interceding

We need to note, again, the role of the Holy Spirit in all of this. When we pray, the Holy Spirit is very active and at work in our lives. He helps us to pray, He intercedes on our behalf when we can't, He gives us the language when we don't know what to pray. Praying without the Spirit can cause prayer to be much harder work than Jesus intended it to be. If prayer is ultimately about connecting with the Father who knows us and loves us, then He is not going to expect us to have to strain in that connection; wrestle sometimes perhaps, but not strain. He wants our communication with Him to be natural, honest, free and easy. There are times prayer can be tough, but looking back over my own prayer life I can see that those harder times were the ones when I have tried to pray in my own strength. The times when prayer has felt most natural, have been the times when I have begun my prayers with this prayer: 'Holy Spirit, help me to pray what is on the heart of the Father.' If the Holy Spirit is for us today what Jesus was to His disciples, then we can just as easily ask the Spirit the same question the disciples asked of Jesus; 'Lord, teach us to pray' (Luke 11:1).

I think the concept of groans can fall into both or either of these two categories – crying in pain or praying in tongues – or there may be other things that Paul was implying, but the fundamental thing to remember is that we needn't pray alone when praying for difficult things, because the Spirit Himself, the same one who raised Jesus from the dead, is interceding for us, with groans too deep for words. Not just through us, not just with us, but incredibly, *for* us. I don't know about you but I am always encouraged when I hear someone say that they pray for me. There have been times in my life when I have been very aware of people praying for me, and I have known others to testify to that during very difficult times. As great as it is to know that someone you know is praying for you, it is even more so to know that God Himself, the Holy Spirit is praying for you! If you ever feel alone, or out of your depth, or you feel like God has forgotten you – look to this verse and remember that He has not forgotten you, or abandoned you, but is interceding for you with groans too deep for words. On top of this, look around you at your church, your community, the people you love, the people you find it difficult to love, because He is interceding for them too. When you pray for the world, you are joining in with prayers the Spirit is already praying. Let's join Him more, even if it means wailing, weeping, crying, silence, speaking in tongues, because in doing so a powerful, world-changing connection is taking place.

I encourage you to think about an issue that you have been struggling to pray for recently, or perhaps something that you know when you pray for you are just going through the motions. With that thing/person/place in mind, find a quiet space and pray the simple prayer at the end of this chapter – then just wait. Be open to whatever the Spirit may want to do as you join with Him in intercession. You may feel nothing, sense nothing, hear nothing or say nothing – this doesn't mean, however, that nothing is happening. Even in the silence, by consciously doing so, you will be interceding with the Spirit.

Holy Spirit, help me to pray what is on the heart of the Father. Amen!

14 MORE THAN CONQUERORS

No, in all these things we are more than conquerors through him who loved us.

-8:37-

I used to love kayaking. At school we had an amazing physics teacher who would teach us how to kayak in after-school clubs. We would also go down to the local river on Saturdays, and occasionally have kayaking weekends where we would camp and kayak and share stories, and our teacher would teach us about the night sky through his love of astronomy. Mr. Hawthorn, although in his late 50s at the time, was fearless. He had done inspiring things through his life including kayaking down a waterfall! He would always try to inspire that sense of adventure and fearlessness in us. To do this, in the winter months he would teach us, in the school swimming pool, how to roll a kayak. It was important for us to learn how to conquer capsizing without having to get out of the kayak. It is a physically hard manoeuvre, and it is easy to panic once you are under the water, and in that state of panic, to forget what it is you are supposed to be doing, but it is a great feeling when you achieve your first roll. He then taught us how to roll without our paddles, just in case we ever found ourselves in a situation that would require us to know how to do that.

Little did we know at the time, he was teaching us these skills because he had a plan in mind. One Saturday whilst gently ambling up the river we came to a footbridge. We would often stop at this point for a rest. As was normal, we pulled our kayaks out of the water and sat on the bank. Mr Hawthorn, however, did not join us. He carried his kayak to the bridge. He placed it on top on the bridge railings, carefully climbed in then launched himself off the bridge. His kayak nose-dived into the river then flipped upside down. Seconds later, using his advanced rolling skills, he was the right way up with a huge smile on his face, and he turned to us and said, "Your turn."

Although we were all fairly confident in our rolling abilities, this seemed a step too far, for me at least. A friend of mine who was with us, lived for moments like this and was straight up on that bridge and successfully and joyfully completing the manoeuvre. After a few more people had a go, it was my turn. I had to conquer some nerves, and to remember the conquering I had already achieved in the pool earlier in the year. Eventually (after a little push from a friend) I launched off. Once I conquered my fear and the challenge, the experience brought me a new-found freedom. I think we ended up being there for about an hour as we launched again, and again, and again.

Conquerors

William the Conqueror is a name that I am sure many would be familiar with, even if, like me, history is not your main subject. The ruthless and merciless leadership of this Norman king led him to conquer and defeat the King of England, and to claim the crown as his own. Stories like this, and other world leaders, who have used their power to conquer kingdoms and nations, have sometimes led to there being a slightly negative tinge to the word. We don't often see conquering as a positive thing, except perhaps in the context of conquering our fears. But the word 'conquerors' that appears in many of our English translations today may not fully do justice to Paul's original intentions for the word. A more accurate translation of the Greek word used is the word 'overcome'. More specifically it can be translated, as William D. Mounce reveals as '[to] be victorious in a struggle'.[13]

We all know that facing struggles is a fact of life; in fact it is a promise of Jesus that suffering and struggle will come to us and that we will suffer because of His name, that persecution, for example, is a matter of course for those who choose to follow Him (see Matthew 10:22, 24:9, John 15:21, 2 Timothy 3:12). Suffering and struggle are symptoms of a broken and fallen world that none of us can escape. Whilst it may seem that some struggle more than others, we do all have times of struggle. Saying 'yes' to Jesus doesn't mean that suffering and struggle will be alleviated. As someone who had been shipwrecked, imprisoned and punished for his faith in Christ, Paul himself would have been all too aware of that reality.

The issue of suffering remains one of the greatest stumbling blocks to many who are on the fringes of faith in Christ. 'If God is all-loving, why does He allow suffering?' Many have tried to answer this, but as explored earlier in this book, I am yet to come across and full and perfect answer. I think this may well continue to be a mystery this side of heaven, a painful mystery, but a mystery nonetheless. Personally, however, I don't think that being a Christian, or being more than a conqueror, is about knowing the answer to the suffering question, but rather it is about knowing some key things when suffering and struggle come.

1. Who God is

I hope that it has been made clear throughout this book that there is a huge need for us as Christians to ensure that we have a large enough picture of who God is, and of what He can do. Take creation, for example. The creation story is a joy to read and fun to teach kids, but I have known many people who struggle over whether it should be taken literally or seen as a metaphor. The reality is we weren't there when it happened, but we trust scripture to be God breathed and inspired (2 Timothy 3:16). For me, though, the question isn't 'Did God create the world in seven days?' but rather the question should be 'Do I believe that he could have?' In other words, 'Is my vision of God big enough to believe that he could have created the world the way that the writer of Genesis describes?'

Or, take my absolute favourite Old Testament story – the valley of dry bones in Ezekiel 37. It is an incredible scene and I urge you read it. Again, commentators have argued for it being a metaphor, or a dream or vision. Again, I believe that if your mind doesn't let you believe that those dry bones could have really come back to life and formed a living breathing army, then your vision of God is not big enough. If your vision of God isn't big enough, then you will never truly believe the words of Matthew 19:26: 'with God all things are possible'.

It is really important in the context of being more than conquerors, to understand how big God is. The reason is to do with victory. To be a conqueror you have to either be victorious or to be on the side that is – our God is victorious and He reigns. He reigns over all and He is seated high on the throne, and yet He – this victorious, powerful, majestic God – has adopted us into His family and given us the inheritance of His kingdom, through His son. We are, ultimately, on the winning side with a victorious God, who can do anything, for whom nothing is impossible. A God who has

conquered the two very things that were separating us from Him –
our sin and the symptom of that sin, death – both of which He
annihilated at the cross and resurrection of his Son, Jesus. He has
the victory. He is the one who has conquered. It is like being signed
up to join a sporting team who have already secured enough points
to win the league – whatever happens, whatever we lose from this
point, will have no lasting effect on what we have already gained in
Christ. Jesus is enough for us. We have a relationship with this
magnificent, amazing, awesome, powerful, all-knowing, all-loving,
conquering God. He is our Father God! Just try to tell me there is
any better security to be found than that.

2. God's Experience of Suffering

In the current Alpha film series, presenter Toby Flint shares
a story of his father's death after eight years of suffering from
dementia. He emotionally and powerfully describes how Jesus'
suffering on the cross, and knowing that God himself has suffered
and knows what it is to suffer, made sense of his own suffering. To
know that in suffering God is with us, alongside us, makes a huge
difference to us.[14]

God is able to speak into our suffering, not just from a
sympathetic point of view, but from the point of view of someone
who has himself experienced suffering, so is able to empathise,
which is far more powerful. You will know the difference between
sympathy and empathy if you have ever tried to support someone,
or have been supported by someone, when you have lived through
similar experiences. There is a different level of understanding when
an experience has been shared by two people – and our God has an
incredible amount of experience of suffering. He is, therefore, able
to relate to the pain we feel in a way that is unique to someone who
has experienced that pain. This is important to remember when we

are suffering and struggling because it helps us to conquer, knowing that beside us is one who has conquered.

In fact, when Paul is saying that we are more than conquerors, he does not say that this is the case when we have come through difficult times. He does not say that we are more than conquerors when we are able to rise above suffering, because he knows we can't always do that. He does not even say that we are more than conquerors through our suffering. What he says quite clearly is that *in* all these things we are more than conquerors. What that means is that we won't truly know what it means to be more than a conqueror until we have experienced suffering and seen that it is possible to hold on to God through that suffering. It is in times of hardship, persecution, famine and sword that we are able to be more than conquerors through Christ, in whose suffering we share.

3. The Choice we Have

Knowing these truths is one thing, but we still have a choice when suffering comes. As a vicar in the Church of England, I often conduct funerals. This ministry is a huge privilege and one I never take for granted. The thing I have found over the years is that whatever the circumstances of the person's passing, the people they leave behind tend to suffer. It is always difficult to witness this suffering as it takes many different forms. I have also noticed, however, that there is a stark difference in how suffering is faced by those who have faith in Jesus and those who don't. Whilst, for many, there will be a temptation to blame God for 'taking a loved one away' or for 'allowing' that tragedy to happen, for the Christian, there is more often than not an acknowledgement of a choice we have. Regardless of not having all the answers to all the 'why' questions, that choice is a simple one: to face suffering with God or without Him. I often wonder how, but people do face suffering without God.

But those who choose to face it with Him, discover His compassion, His comfort, His peace, His presence, His gentleness, His understanding, His empathy, and the hope that He gives, are a huge strength and comfort in the face of suffering. These things may not be apparent at the time, but all those people who I know to have genuine faith, will testify to knowing some, or all of these things at some point in their grief and suffering – this is the aforementioned steadiness that God can provide, because He is a conqueror.

As well as this, there is the hope beyond this life. For the person who has passed this life, if they had faith in Jesus, their death is merely a change of address. For the person left behind, if they have faith, there is the hope of their own eternity with Jesus, and the certainty of knowing that their loved one is with Him. In 2018 we lost one of the great men of recent Christian history. Billy Graham's passion for the gospel and his gift in delivering it led to many people the world over coming to faith. As is often the case these days when someone of his renown passes away, social media became full of quotes attributed to him. One such quote by Billy Graham perfectly sums up this concept of hope in death: 'Someday you will read or hear that Billy Graham is dead. Don't you believe a word of it. I shall be more alive than I am now. I will just have changed my address. I will have gone into the presence of God.'[15]

Facing suffering and grief well, for the Christian, is not about having all the answers to all of life's questions, but is rather about a shift in perspective – this is what makes us more than conquerors when suffering comes, and all that is possible because we are in a living relationship with a God who Himself has suffered but has conquered over that suffering and even over death itself. This is a God who is in the business of turning crucifixions into resurrections. A God who is the source of all hope, life and love. A God who has given us a certain and secure hope of a better place. A God who will wipe away every tear and all the pain (Revelation 21:4).

A God who stands with us in our suffering, walks with us through the valley. A God whose love is sufficient and powerful. That is why, when we are in Christ, and He is in us, we are able to say boldly that we are more than conquerors.

4. Love vs Separation

Another important thing for us to remember when suffering comes is the fact that suffering need not cause separation; in fact, it can't. In 8:36, Paul is making it clear that there is nothing that can separate us from the love of Christ. He lists a lot of realities, things that are very real to us. He is not just listing spiritual things that we face, but he is giving very real-life examples. He speaks of trial, distress, persecution, famine, sword, nakedness, peril. These are things that can affect our entire beings, our entire identities. We are trinitarian beings, made of body, mind and spirit, created in the image of a trinitarian God. And each part of us is important, each making us who we are, and this list of the things that we can overcome covers it all – the physical problems, the emotional pain, the mental breakdown, the spiritual opposition. None of these attacks, none of these real-life problems, no matter what their root, can separate us from the love of Christ. Even if we *feel* separated, it is impossible for us to actually be separated from His love.

Persecution is something that all of us experience on some level but let us not forget that Paul is writing to a church that is right in the middle of experiencing violent persecution, as an everyday reality. Paul himself is probably writing whilst under house arrest for proclaiming Jesus – but this has not separated him from the love of Christ.

Paul refers to famine, and he is likely to be referring to physical famine caused by the poverty that would have been prominent in parts of Rome. I have had the privilege of being in

Africa with people so poor that they have no idea where their next meal was going to come from. These people have shown more generosity than anyone else I have known anyone with wealth to show – their famine has not separated them from the love of Christ.

When Adam and Eve first sinned, their shame caused them to be aware of their nakedness and to cover up, and then they hid, but our nakedness, our shame, the things we would rather not expose to others, the things we are ashamed of, those parts of us we want to keep hidden – they cannot separate us from the love of Christ.

Being a Christian does not exempt us from these things of life, and as hard as these things may be, and even though they may cause our faith to falter or wobble, they may cause us to have to cling on to our faith with our fingertips, they may even cause us to walk away from our faith for a while, but they will not change how much God loves us. When all else fails, love remains (see 1 Corinthians 13).

The enemy's main aim in life is to separate us from Christ. He may, at times, succeed on some levels, but the one thing he will never succeed in, no matter what tactics he may try, is separating us from the love of God that is in Christ Jesus!

Have you ever been lost? I don't recall ever being lost but there was one time when I was in primary school that one of my parents lost track of time and was very late picking me up. I had to wait outside the school office whilst the teachers tried to get hold of my parents (in the days before mobile phones), to find out where they were. After what seemed like forever, but in reality, was probably only about 20 minutes, my mum came rushing in and collected me. Relief, not only for me, but also for my teachers who thought they may have had to find another way of getting me home. That brief moment of unplanned separation was painful and scary.

There is always a huge sense of relief and often joy when we are reunited with something or someone that we have lost. We love connection and are made to be in connection. When we lose connection, for whatever reason, we feel as though something is wrong. Consider the empty nest syndrome when the last child goes to university, or that moment we say goodbye to someone we love. It is hard to be separated from the ones we love. Many people experienced this to the extreme during national lockdowns.

There are plenty of Bible stories that show this and the pain that separation can cause families split apart by conflict, family feuds, death and many other factors. These are all stories we find in God's great narrative. These issues are still very much a reality today; it is something we see almost every day in our news as we see more and more people displaced from their homes.

It should hardly be surprising though, because the overall narrative of the Bible is our separation from God and His mission to bring us back into relationship with Him. It is an amazing story of God showing grace, redemption, forgiveness, reconciliation, mercy, kindness, goodness, justice, miracles, opportunities, battles (spiritual and physical), pain, heartache, sorrow, patience, incarnation, the death of His son, power, resurrection and so much more, to bring us back into relationship – and all despite Him being rejected time and time again by His people. The story reveals that He still thinks that you and I are worth all of that! It stands to reason that when a child of His repents and chooses Jesus, chooses life with Him, chooses to enter back into relationship, He is not going to let that child out of His love – though to be honest, we never have been. The earlier reflection on the prodigal son shows us that whilst He may let us go out from His presence, we cannot go outside of His love.

Nothing you have done, or will do, will stop Him loving you. Nothing you do will make Him love you any less and nothing you do can make Him love you more than He already does. It is painful for us when someone we love chooses life without God, and perhaps even more so when they have known life with Jesus but circumstances have caused them to walk away from that relationship. But God has not given up on them in that moment, He doesn't stop loving them because they made a different choice. He doesn't ignore them, or think they are no longer worth the death that Jesus died for them. He loves them. Unconditionally, He loves them, and the same is true for all of us. Whether or not we feel loved is a different matter, but the truth is you cannot be separated from the love of God. It is a love that is hard to measure or compare to anything else and it is a love that is for you.

The enemy likes to try and distract us away from God's love because knowing that we are loved is a powerful conquering weapon that can withstand most, if not all, things in life. Nothing can separate us from the love of Christ. This love, and all its sufficient power, is what makes us more than conquerors — that is the true power of love when it comes from the God who Himself is love.

More…

It is knowledge of these truths that helps us to know that we are conquerors, but only through Christ. We cannot be conquerors on our own or in our own strength, but in Christ we are. All of these things in life, and even death itself, are not only defeated by God but they serve Him, and therefore us as His children. We are no longer slaves to them. Yes, they may affect us but they won't destroy us. When persecution hits hard, the church often grows stronger than ever. When we are at our weakest, God is able to work His strength from that. When we experience shame, God has the opportunity to show how He destroyed shame on the cross. Even if we experience famine, it provides us with an opportunity to see how God can give us our daily bread and provide for us. Even death itself serves the purpose of bringing us into eternity with Jesus. Because of this reality, death is now a servant of God. Death serves His purpose of uniting us for eternity This is what makes us more than conquerors. I believe that one of the greatest witnesses to this world is the Christian who holds fast to God and stands on the knowledge of these truths, in the face of suffering. That makes people take notice, because the world knows it needs that kind of hope, that kind of love, that kind of connection, that kind of God.

What Paul is summing up here is that because of the truths of Romans 8:1, 2, 5, 9, 15, 18, 20, 21, 25, 26, 28 and 31 that we have explored in this book (albeit we have only scratched the surface) along with all the other verses in between, and the gospel of the God of love that they are all about, we can be more than conquerors in the things we face in life – all, and only, because we are children who know the Father, live in Christ and are filled with the Spirit.

Father, thank you that nothing can separate me from your love.

Thank you that because of who you are, and because I am yours, I am more than a conqueror.

Thank you that no matter what life throws at me, no matter what the enemy tries to do, and even when I come to my last – nothing will separate me from the love that you have for me.

Help me to believe and to walk in the truth that I am more than a conqueror through Christ, who loves me. Amen!

15 LIVING THE ROMANS 8 LIFE

Without some application, this book would be no more than a study of a small section of biblical text, but as the title suggests, the hope has been for these words to provide more than that. It is important for me to begin this final chapter by stating that I, in no way, consider myself to be an expert in living a Romans 8 life. The journey of writing this book has been a challenge to me in that I have been reminded, often, of where I am failing to live this life, but it has also reminded me of the fact that that's okay. These are life-transforming verses from Paul, and whilst some of that transformation is instant, some transformation will take more time. But God doesn't only love the finished article – He still loves this 'work in progress' son of His. I want to finish, however, with a few practical things that may help us to live the Romans 8 Life.

Read Often

I am of course primarily talking about reading scripture at this stage but I want to expand on that a little. The word of God is a wonderful and precious gift to us as His people. Whilst this is a study on one particular chapter of the Bible, I hope I have made it clear how important I believe the whole of scripture to be in our discipleship. Romans 8 is a beautifully-crafted summary of our faith and of God's salvation plan, but it needs its wider context. Yes, it may be the Mount Everest but we need to be mindful that Everest sits within a bigger picture of the Himalayas and that they sit in an even bigger picture of a bigger, wider world. Getting to know that wider context for ourselves helps us to truly grasp the wonder of what Paul has written.

As well as reading scripture itself I am a firm believer that theological study is for all Christian disciples, not just for those who go to university or college. Theology is the study of the word of God – something which we should all be doing. There are some that would argue that the Bible is all we need. In many senses they are correct but I am yet to meet anyone who professes to know and understand everything about God's word. Wisdom and understanding and knowledge can come in many forms and one of them is through the wisdom of others.

When we read the Bible, there will inevitably be things about it we don't understand, or perhaps even struggle to agree with. When we come across such texts, we are faced with a choice: to ignore it and move on and skip over it whenever we come across it again, or to seek to understand. We have the opportunity to wrestle with the word and its meaning for us personally and for the church. There are times we can do this through prayer and asking God. There are times we can do this through discussion with others. As an external processor, one of my favourite places on earth was the common room at my theological college in Bristol. I loved coming down from an afternoon of writing or lectures and (after a game or two of table football) processing my thoughts and arguments with others, and often gaining fresh insights and perspectives from my peers. But again, this isn't just something for theological college. There are people I know I can call or arrange to have coffee with if I come across something in God's word that I know I need to process, and I urge you to have people like this in your life too.

To go back to the Mount Everest analogy (in the hope I am not taking it too far) – if you were to climb Everest you would need other experts with you, often people who have climbed it before. Also, when climbing Everest, you would need to climb a distance and come back down to a base camp as your body adjusted to changes in climate. This is true also with our reading Romans 8. We may, for example, read verse one and think 'yep I get that,' but once we get to the stuff about the Spirit of freedom, we perhaps need to take a climb back down again to find out what others may have said about that subject. If we are struggling to really accept our identity as adopted children of God, then we need to read books on that subject. For example, the story of the prodigal son took on so much more meaning for me when I read about the culture of the time and the significance of what Jesus was teaching his disciples. This wasn't at theological college but was in a book about the father heart of God.

I am aware that it is all very well me saying 'read more' but some may see this as an unachievable concept. The question becomes then: how do I read more? How much should I read? What does *reading more* look like in my life? Well generally I would say that it is a good idea to seek to read a little more than you already do.

If you currently do not read the Bible at all then you may be feeling a sense of shame about that. The best way to combat that shame is to start reading (again). Be realistic about the expectations that you have of yourself. Start with something familiar. Romans 8 perhaps, or even a chapter of Mark's gospel each day, or try reading a psalm a day. I often find that the more I read, the more I want to read, but it is also about creating healthy habits. I talked about addictions earlier. We can't just cut out addictions, we need to replace the neuro pathways with new ones, so it is about creating healthy addictions – and reading God's word is one very healthy thing to get addicted to. But we need to ensure that our reading is not driven by obligation. It is good to ask, 'Why do I want to read the Bible?' If your answer is something like 'I really want to get to know God better' then you are on the right track. It may only be a chapter or a few verses a day, but any reading is better than no reading.

If you are someone who already reads regularly, then ask yourself and God if there are any passages or books of the Bible you know you always try to avoid? If so, could you read one today and begin to wrestle with it? Perhaps read around it, read what others have said about it, and if possible discuss it with others.

Perhaps you read regularly but your reading has become more about routine and less about relationship. Maybe you could try something new with your reading. You could try reading a different version or translation of scripture, perhaps listen to an audio version, use a study guide that takes you through a particular theme, read with others, read aloud – try something new, and ask again, 'what is my motive for reading this?'

Regardless of how much you currently read, where you read and when you read, don't forget to read with the Holy Spirit. Our kids are all bookworms, they all love to read. They can sit with their heads in a book quite happily for hours. When they are reading I have no idea what is going on in their heads, what they are thinking or feeling, how they are reacting to what they read. Sometimes though I get to read to them or with them. When we do this, they might stop to ask me questions about a meaning of a word (which when reading on their own they may simply skip over), or they may stop to ask me what I think about what that character just did or said. They might ask me to clarify something we read earlier. We enjoy and study the text together and have a very different reading experience.

Now imagine doing that kind of reading with the author who wrote the book. As a child, I would have loved the opportunity to sit down with Roald Dahl and to ask him how he came up with his ideas, what his inspirations were and how he came up with 'scrumptitious' made-up words. We can do this with the Bible. We have the opportunity to sit down with its author and ask Him to read it with us. We can have Him answer our questions, explain His meaning, show us more than we could ever discover ourselves – why would we ever not want that?!

Pray Freely

Prayer is, by far, one of the greatest gifts of God to His people. The God who is holy, majestic, all righteous, all powerful, high above all – invites us into an open dialogue with Him. A dialogue that not only we *can* enter into whenever we like, but we are in fact *invited* to do so, always and 'without ceasing' (1 Thessalonians 5:16-17).

Whilst prayer is not unique to Christianity, the status we have when we pray is unique. Being able to approach God as our father has a level of intimacy about it that has never been known before between a deity and his/her people, let alone the relationship between the one true living God, YHWH, and His people. It's a posture of prayer that shocked the religious authorities in Jesus' time and one that is still incomparable today.

This intimacy is the one that Jesus not only encouraged us, but also commanded us, to use when we pray. This shows that something radically changes as a result of his incarnation and later death and resurrection. He gives us the right, the restoration of relationship needed through dealing with our sin, that allows as to call God 'our Father'. When that curtain of the temple was violently torn in two (see Mark 15:38) it was God's way of saying: 'now you can approach, now you can come close, now intimacy between us is allowed again. I can walk in the garden with you again. Not only can I know you but you can know me, through my son.'

We must never lose the sense of privilege and wonder when it comes to prayer but we also know that we can approach Him as we are, whenever, wherever and however we like. He will always be patient with us, attentive to us. When we pray we will be the most important thing to Him in that moment and we will have His full attention. Even more remarkably, He will also want to speak to us.

There'll be times prayer is hard, but Romans reminds us that the Spirit can intercede, with, for and through us with groans too deep for words if necessary. There will be times prayer feels like a fight, but wrestle through. Our prayer life can be influenced by so many things around us, but whatever we are feeling, thinking, experiencing – even if we are angry, upset, disillusioned, fed up – we can and we must keep the channels of communication open between us and our Father, in the knowledge that He hears us and He will answer, and we can always ask His Spirit to help us in prayer.

Part of living the Romans 8 life is about not losing this sense of wonder when it comes to prayer. It is about knowing that because of what Jesus did for us, we can approach God in prayer. There is no right or wrong way to pray, there is no better way to pray – it is about connecting with God in a way that is 'you shaped' and knowing that you have His full attention. Never lose the wonder of the fact that you, as His son/daughter, can talk to the God who made everything, whenever you like. As well as that, if you listen, He may even have some things to say to you! And remember that when you pray you are joining in with the interceding that the Spirit is already doing.

Walk with the Spirit

Having explored earlier in this book the powerful reality of the Spirit of God dwelling in us, the question is 'what does it mean to walk with the Spirit?' He is always around us, and inside us but to walk with him, to my mind, is to be intentional in a different way. You will have probably heard phrases like 'I just want to join in with what the Spirit is doing' or 'show me Lord where you are working'. I remember someone teaching me to pray each day, 'Good morning Holy Spirit what shall we do today?' I love this concept because it is about intentionally wanting to work in partnership with the Holy Spirit. This acknowledges first that He is a *He* and we can work with *Him*. It shows our dependence on Him, even for the simplest of tasks. I also find it means that I notice Him more. There are things that He does each and every day that most of the time we completely miss or don't recognise as being the work of the Spirit. If, however, we are consciously acknowledging Him at the start of the day, then we can begin to see His leading, His gentle guiding. We may begin to think differently about situations, we begin to see people how God sees them, we begin to desire the things He desires and to dislike the things He dislikes, and to prioritise what is a priority to Him.

I am not saying that these things don't happen anyway, of course they do because God is gracious and has a habit of trying to get our attention – but I think walking in the Spirit is about Him not needing to gain our attention because He already has it. We need to ask ourselves how many burning bushes do we walk past every day because we are simply too distracted to see them? Sure, we will still get distracted, life will still happen, things will still get in the way, things will still be hard at times, but if He already has our attention from the start of the day, then we can see more of Him throughout that day – even in the smallest of things. All I want in my life is to try my best to make sure that I don't miss anything God wants to use to encourage me, challenge me, shape me, mould me, grow me, change me and help me to become the best version of myself that I can be – more like Christ. I acknowledge I need Him for this. I want to work with Him. I want to partner with the Spirit who lives in me and is around me. I want to find Him in the small things and the big things. At the times I find I am able to do this, I appreciate more, life is more joyful and exciting. The challenges of life are still there but I know, without a shadow of a doubt, that I am not facing them alone.

If things are hard for you right now, I can understand how alien this may sound, and how unachievable it may appear to be. You may be reading this and thinking, 'well it's alright for you but *this* hasn't happened to *you*.' I do not deny that it is easier to do this when we are in a good place. When we are in that good place, and all is well with our souls, this is the best place to practise this, for when the going does get tougher. Anyone who has ever struggled with anger, for example, will be able to tell you that there are so many strategies you can use to calm down, but the best time to practise these strategies is actually when you are calm. Any married couple will know that when things are going really well is the best time to get marriage counselling, to read books and to invest in your marriage for when harder seasons or life's challenges come your way.

It is like this too when it comes to walking with the Spirit. Every day we have the opportunity to get up and go through a day with the Holy Spirit! He invites us to partner with Him. He has come to be our counsellor, our guide, to be to us what Jesus was to His disciples. If Jesus was right in front of you right now asking you to spend the day with Him I am sure you wouldn't think twice about saying yes (regardless of how you are feeling right now) – well in truth He is. Every day the Holy Spirit (the Spirit of Jesus) is saying to us, 'Will you walk with me today?' Why would we not want to do that?!

Remember Whose you are

It can be a difficult thing to truly believe that we are who God says we are. Scripture, and particularly this chapter in Romans, makes it incredibly clear that we are adopted, chosen, precious children of God. It is important that we remind ourselves of this truth on a regular basis. We may need to preach it to ourselves regularly. Sharing it with others also helps to remind us and placing ourselves in places where this truth is taught – whether through song, spoken word or fellowship – can also aid us. It can be as simple as saying aloud each day, 'I am chosen by God' or 'I am a son/daughter of God.'

This is who are you, this is who God says you are. This is the one truth that the enemy will do all he can to make you doubt, question or even forget. There will be times you have to let the devil know; 'not today!' and to speak the truth of your God-given identity over your own life again. We can never hear about it too much, we can never read about it too often. It needs to become a lived truth. More than just an idea, but something we believe at the core of who we are. If there is anything stopping that from being the case for you today then do whatever it takes for you to be able to truly believe it. Pray with others, get counselling if you need to. Whatever it takes, we need to know, believe and live the truth that we are children of God – only made possible by what Christ did on the cross. You are His beloved! Preach this gospel to yourself every day.

Prioritise Rest

There is nothing quite like resting in the presence of God. Times when there is no agenda, no list of requests and petitions, no pressures weighing on our minds – just resting in the presence of God. I hope that all readers have experienced this at least once in their lives. The reality is that a huge majority of Christians struggle with this concept because they feel guilty, feel they should be *doing* rather than being. It's the (all too common) Martha syndrome (Luke 10:38-42) or older son mentality that was discussed earlier in this book.

People can confuse rest with being idle. But resting in God's presence is not being idle any more than spending quality time with any loved one is. There are times when you have someone close to you – a spouse, family member or good friend – where just being with them can be enough to strengthen your relationship. Words may not be needed. There may be silence, but it won't feel awkward – so it should be between us and God. To be in His presence should be enough.

We always need to ask if God is enough for us. If He is not then something needs to change. Whilst I agree there are things that need to be done in life, there are things that we need to stay on top of, there is no greater priority in our life than spending time with God. He should be our absolute priority over everything else.

I don't know if you are the kind of person who writes 'to do' lists for your day's tasks. Even if you are not that kind of person you are likely to, on some level, process through the things that you need to do. At the very top of that list should be these three items:

1. Love God more
2. Know Jesus better
3. Rely on the Holy Spirit

If it gets to the end of the day and we have been unable to tick those three items off then something has gone wrong in our day – somewhere the balance has been off. Something, be it our work, our family, our tasks, has become more important than seeking God. This isn't something that should make us feel guilty or obliged to 'have a quiet time' but the reality is there is nothing more important in this life that knowing God more and loving Jesus better, and we rely on His Spirit to help us in this. This is what our lives and identity are about.

Prioritising rest in God's presence shows that there is nothing more important in our lives than Him. By seeking to rest in His presence above anything else is the living out of the belief that He is the bread of life, the living water, the first and last – our everything. He is all we need in life, and anything else that we have outside of the presence of God is an added bonus. This isn't just some nice ideal that we can't possibly obtain – this is what we were made for.

This is about 'seeking His presence'. Seeking His presence for the sake of seeking His presence – not because we want the 'added benefits'. We may want to see healing, to witness the miraculous, to know His provision, to see our prayers answered, to see revival or to personally grow in the fruits. None of these things are bad things to want and we know that none of these things are possible without or outside of His presence – but these things, (despite Paul's urging to eagerly desire them), should not be *the* reasons for wanting to be in His presence. I want to be in His presence because I love being with Him.

There are times my kids spend time with me because we are doing something together. There are times that my kids spend time with me because there is something they want. There are times my kids spend time with me because they know they should. But by far the best times for me as a father are the times when a child climbs into my lap just because they want to be with me, to know my embrace, to feel safe and loved. It delights me as a father. I wonder how God feels when we choose His presence for the sake of choosing His presence, because as His children we just want to be with our Daddy and we know there is no better, safer or more privileged place to be!

What God does when we are in His presence is up to Him. We may have our requests, our hopes, our dreams and we can certainly bring them with us when we seek His presence, but prioritising rest is about His presence being enough, His presence being more important than those dreams or desires. It's about gaining a right perspective on life. There is no better place from which to view our life than from the lap of our Father God!

Reflect on His Faithfulness

The truth is that God is always good. He has always been a good father and He always will be because 'His love endures for ever' (Psalm 136). We often need to remind ourselves of this fact and there are a number of ways we can do this:

1. Read the promises of God regularly. There are thousands of promises in the Bible made by God and He has never broken a single one. Take some time to find them and read them. Perhaps find a study guide that takes you through all the promises of God. Ask people what their favourite promise of God is. There are so many to choose from. Some of the promises are outrageous and it is amazing to read of their fulfilment. Look, for example, at all the promises made through the prophets of a Messiah, then see just how amazingly they are fulfilled in the person of Jesus Christ.

2. Remember His faithfulness to you. We all go through difficult times, times when it feels like God has forgotten us or abandoned us. These dry and barren times are an important part of our Christian life. In these times we need to try to reflect back (not to dwell) on the past. We can all remember times when God has been really faithful to us. When we have seen that answer to prayer, or experienced

His incredible provision, or had that fresh encounter with Him, or that time of worship where we really connected. If nothing else, we have all been saved by grace and given life and forgiveness of sin. It is important to look back on these times where God has done something in our lives that only God can do and to remember that He is the same God now as He was then. He is still faithful. He is still good. He is still God. Remember that you are still loved as much as you were then. You are still as precious. You are still His child. He still wants the best for you. You are still loved. You may not feel it or sense it, but this is where He is working things together for your good. Remember His faithfulness. Read those old journals (if you are someone who keeps a journal). Reminisce with people who were there when events happened. Get back to your first love. He is still that good.

3.   Be encouraged by the experience of others. I love reading biographies of people who have had amazing experiences, or who have had an important influence on society or the church. I love this because it is rare that you would read about a life of these saints without seeing their brokenness and their need to trust and depend on God absolutely. As Matt Redman states in his book *Mirror Ball*, 'Great men and women of God in the past were as dependent on the power of God to strengthen them in their weakness as we are here today'.[16] In their good times we read of God's faithfulness *and* in their darker times still we read of God's faithfulness. Their stories can encourage us, inspire us, challenge us, move us to want more of God in our lives, shake us out of our comfort zones. They remind us that their God is the same as our God and that God was good for them, in the good times and the bad, and so He will be good for us.

As well as reading about the saints, it is good to hear from our peers. I value hugely the role of testimonies in the life of the church. If you are reading this as a person with leadership responsibility of a church that does not include testimonies, even on an occasional basis, then I urge you to ask why that is. Testimonies are important for building up the people of God. We have to take risks to allow testimonies in our churches, but if we allow fear of what might go wrong to prevent us from giving space for testimony at all, then we could end up missing out on the stories of the faithful saints whose genuine desire is to glorify God, testify to His goodness and to build up their brothers and sisters in the process.

If your church doesn't make time for testimony, then make time in small groups, even over coffee with some Christian friends or family. It can be so important to hear about God's work in other people's lives, and to miss out on that can mean that stories that have always been intended to be shared get forgotten or go unnoticed – meaning that something that could have given God glory or that could have helped someone else in their journey has been put under a bushel. Stories of God's goodness and faithfulness can change atmospheres, build hope and faith and even transform lives – because God is good. In her book *Play with Fire,* Bianca Juarez Olthoff says 'When we forget about What God has done, it makes us doubt what he can do'.[17] So let's make sure we remember and remind ourselves and others of His goodness. Paul does this a great deal in his writings when he testifies to what God has done in his own life as he has frequently seen God work all things together for his good and the good of others.

If you do Nothing Else...

And with every single verse of Romans 8, next time you read it, ask yourself some very 'simple' questions. Do I believe (and I mean truly believe) this verse and all that it means for me as a child of God? Do I really believe there is no condemnation? Do I really believe that I am an heir of the Kingdom? Do I honestly believe that I can know freedom? Do I pray as though the Spirit is praying with me, through me and for me? Do I really believe, even if I don't feel it or see it, that He is working all things together for my good? Can I honestly say that He is the God that He says He is and that I am who He says I am? If I can just begin to believe those things then they are life-transforming declarations of identity and if I embrace them then I can live life as a precious, chosen, died for, adored, kingdom-inheriting, conquering, adopted child of the living God.

If I can truly believe that I am Saved,

If I can truly believe that I am Adopted,

If I can truly believe that I am Free,

then I can live the Romans 8 life!

ENDNOTES

Introduction

[1] Keller, Timothy: *Romans 8-16 for you* (UK: The Good Book Company, 2015) p. 7

[2] Packer, J. I.: *Knowing God* (Hodder and Stoughton, 1975) p. 284

[3] Packer, J. I.: *Knowing God* (Hodder and Stoughton, 1975) p. 284

Chapter 1

[4] For further reading around this subject see: Stone, D. & Gregory, D.: *The Rest of the Gospel* (Harvest House Publishers, 2014)

[5] Tchividjian, Tullian: Jesus + Nothing = Everything (Crossway, 2011) p. 140

Chapter 3

[6] A.W. Tozer: *God Tells the Man who Cares* (Authentic 1993) p. 141

Chapter 6

[7] Packer, J. I.: *Knowing God* (Hodder and Stoughton, 1975) p. 224

[8] Lucado, Max: *Just Like Jesus* (Thomas Nelson, 2003) p. xi

[9] Ash, Christopher: *Introducing Romans* (Christian Focus Publications, 2013) p. 77

[10] Tchividjian, Tullian: *Jesus + Nothing = Everything* (Crossway, 2011) p. 103

Chapter 11

[11] Woolridge, Rachel (HTB Sunday Sermons Podcasts, 5th November 2017)

[12] Source Unknown

[13] Mounce, William D.: *Mounce's Complete Expository Dictionary of Old and New Testament Words* (Zondervan, 2006) p. 493

Chapter 14

[14] Alpha Film Series 2016, session 03: Why Did Jesus Die? (London: Alpha 2016)

[15] Source unknown

Chapter 15

[16] Redman, Matt: *Mirror Ball* (David C. Cook, 2011) p. 50

[17] Juarez Olthoff, Bianca: *Play with Fire: Discovering fierce faith, unquenchable passion, and a life-giving God* (Zondervan, 2016) p. 132

Printed in Great Britain
by Amazon

42644055R00106